Incarnations of Holy Mother
(Different Incarnations of *Śrī Devī*)

*

Dr. Ramamurthy N.

M.Sc., B.G.L., CAIIB, CCP, DSADP, CISA, PMP, CGBL, Ph.D.

*

*****

Title: Incarnations of Holy Mother
                          (Different Incarnations of *Śrī Devī*)

First Edition: 2020

Author: **Dr. Ramamurthy N,**
                          http://ramamurthy.jaagruti.co.in/

Copyright ©:   With the author (No part of this book
                          may be reproduced in any manner
                          whatsoever without the written
                          permission from the author).

Number of pages: 136

ISBN (13):   978-93-82237-68-6

Price: ₹ 200

*****

Table of Contents

*****

Dedication

मातृ देवो भव

या देवी सर्वभूतेषु मातृरूपेण संस्थिता ।
नमस्तस्यै नमस्तस्यै नमस्तस्यै नमो नमः ॥

Mātru Devo Bhava

Yā Devī Sarvabhūteṣu Mātru Rūpena Samstitā |

Namastasyai Namastasyai Namastasyai Namo Namaḥ ||

This book is dedicated with devotion to all the *upasakas* of *Śrī Devī*. There cannot be even an iota of doubt that all will be blessed by *Śrī Ambikai.*

Dr. Ramamurthy N

*****

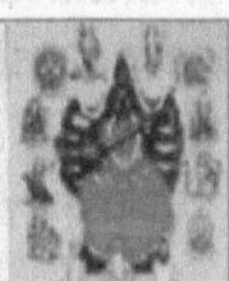

Blessings 1

Śrī Gurubhyo Namaḥ

Dattatreya Hare Kriṣṇa Unmattānanda Dāyakaḥ
Digambara Mune Bāla Piṣaca Jnāna Sāgarā ||

Śāntam Dāntam Tapo Niṣṭam Śāntānanda Yatīśvaram |
Bajāmi Yaminām Śreṣṭam Avadhūtam Aharniśam ||

Satyamekam Lalitākhyam Vastu Tat Advitīyam
Akhaṇḍārtham Param Brahma ||

The universal opinion of the great sages, is the same energy (*shakti*) in the world. It is seen with different names and forms. If there is no energy (*shakti*), everything in this world, will become static. Just to show this to the world, right from *Dattaatreyar* till *Adi Shankara* have installed various *yantras* in *Devi* temples and blessed the entire universe. They have also created the process of *Mantra Maanasa* puja, *Yantra* puja, *Mandala* puja, Image worship, Tantric puja, etc. The purpose of the *Maharishis* is to observe the Guru Sampradaya and perform *japa*, puja, *homam*, etc., to attain *Siddha suddhi* (purity of mind) and worshiping. The goal is to attain the Moksha Empire by attaining enlightenment. Therefore, all those human beings born in this world should be able to perform the shakti Upasana easily. To enable this the great people have installed the incarnations of the Ambikai (Sri Devi), in idol forms in various temples.

We are much pleased to know that Dr. Ramamurthy is very nicely compiling and publishing a book "Incarnations of *Śrī Devī*", in English and "*Ambikayin (Thiru)Avataarangal*" (அம்பிகையின் (திரு)அவதாரங்கள்) in Tamil. This is written in simple language understandable by all common lay men. We pray to Sri Vidya

Mahaasowbhaagya Paraashodashee Devi, to bless all her compassion to him, his family and the readers of this book.

Let everyone enjoy and live happily.

Happiness   Truth   Auspiciousness

Always in the service of *Sri Devi*.

Jaya Jaya Jagamba – Sri Gurudevadatta

With love

Ayyarmalai   श्रीप्रणवानन्द स्वामिनः
2020   Srividya Parambika Trust

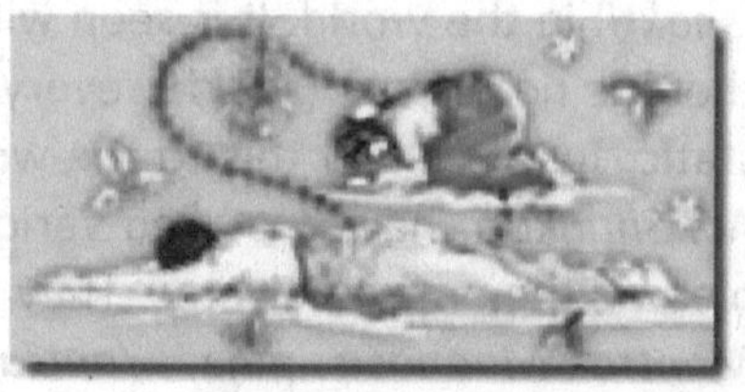

*****

Śrī Śrī Narahari Giri Swamijī
Śrī Samvit Jnānānanda Kendra, Maheshwar,
Śrī Narmadā *Tat*, Madhya Pradesh

Blessings 2

Śrī Gurubhyo Namaḥ

The word *avataram* in Samskrutam means *"Ava Taratee"* – that means Lord comes down from his dwelling place to protect us and to protect the *dharma*. Generally we all know the ten incarnations of Lord *Vishnu*.

Incarnations of Ambikai – The only source of all is Adi Parashakti - this Adi Parashakti is the cause of this creation - that is, Sri Parameswaran created this universe along with Maya (illusion). That illusion is Adi Shakti - Adi Parashakti - Srividya - Brahma Vidya. That same Shakti (power), on account of the differences of the Upadhy, takes many forms and appears to us with different qualities. There are many – many – innumerable incarnations of such holy mother – there are many forms of it. For every form of that mother there are different qualities, some special purpose – Ambikai takes an incarnation in various forms.

In order to explain such incarnations, Dr. Ramamurthy has written this book in a very simple style, trying to be understood by the laity as well.

Usually we worship Rajarajeshwari, Parameswari and Lalita Tripurasundari as the Paradevi of Srividya. There are many goddesses in the same Sriyantra. Similarly in Dasha Maha Vidya there are 10 predominant Devis. Thus according to the protocol of the Goddesses – in that Sriyantra in the posterior triangle, Parameswara-Parameswari or Kameshwara-Kameshwari as a united form – Shiva-shakti is in harmony. That united form is called as Rajarajeshwari. Beneath that, in the Sri Chakra Navavarana, many deities are blessing in each and every enclosure (*avarana*). The source of all these is Adi Parasakthi.

The Sun is only one. Its rays of the sun are one and the same. But they appear and reflect differently as they flow through different media. But that Sun is one and the same. Similarly Adi Parashakti is one and the same. In many places she appears to us in different forms. Whatever the incarnation, the mother is the form of grace. Each incarnation is taken, in order to exalt us, the devotees, to remove our grievances, alleviates our sufferings, gives us eternal bliss and shows us the way to salvation – all the means are gracious to us.

Dr. Ramamurthy has given such special features of different forms of Mother Adiparashakthi in a very simple book a guide-like. We can read this and get to know the Shakta ideology. Just as Advaita realizes the Jiva-Brahma unity, so also Shakta Vidya realizes the Shiva-Shakti harmony. Therefore Shakta and Advaita are one and the same. That Shakta Vidya has been quoted in many a place in this book.

This book has been written in a way that is very easy to comprehend. We pray the Adi Parashakti, for the long life and health of Dr. Ramamurthy to continue his spiritual work tirelessly and for him to publish many more books and guide spiritual lovers on the path to spirituality.

May the grace of Sri Devi be showered pm everyone who reads this book.

Hari Om. Tat Sat.

Camp - Thiruvannamalai

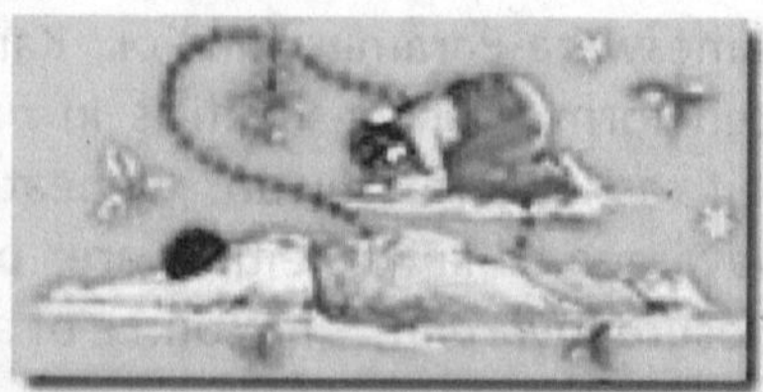

*****

Introduction

ॐ श्री गुरुभ्यो नमः । *Oṃ Śrī Gurubhyo Namaḥ* ।

गुरुर्ब्रह्मा गुरुर्विष्णुः गुरुर्देवो महेश्वरः । गुरु साक्षात् परं ब्रह्म तस्मै श्रीगुरवे नमः ॥

Gururbrahma Gururviṣṇuḥ Gururdevo Maheśvaraḥ ।

Guru Sākśāt Parabrahma Tasmai Śrīgurave Namaḥ ॥

गुरुवे सर्वलोकानां भिषजे भवरोगिनां । निधये सर्व विद्यानां दक्षिण मूर्तिये नमः ॥

Guruve Sarvloksansam Bhiṣaje Bhavaroginām ।

Nidhaye Sarva Vidhyānām Dakśiṇa Mūrtaye Namaḥ ॥

सदाशिव समारंभां शङ्कराचार्य मध्यमां। अस्मद आचार्य पर्यन्तां वन्दे गुरु परंपराम्

Sadāshiva Samārambām Śankarāchārya Madhyamām ।

Asmad Achārya Paranthām Vande Guru Paramparām ॥

श्रुति स्मृति पुराणानामालयं करुणालयम् । नमामि भगवत्पादंशंकरं लोकशंकरम्

Śruti Smruti Purānānām Ālayam Karunālayam ।

Namūmi Bhagavatapādam Śankaram Lokaśankaram ॥

वागर्थाविव सम्प्रुक्तौ वागर्थ प्रतिपत्तये । जगतः पितरौ वन्दे पार्वती परमेश्वरौ ॥

Vāgarthāviva Sampruktakou Vāgartha Pratipaye ।

Jagataḥ Pitarou Vande Pārvati Parameśwarou ॥

We all originated from *Brahmam*[1]. We reach that *Brahmam* – We merge with that *Brahmam*. That is actually *liam-samāti*. This rhythm cannot be exercised without the use or support of an appropriate instructor. The *Upasana* is aimed at an idol. It is both *Saguna* (with qualities) and (without qualities) *Nirguna*. A person is capable of doing *Nirguna Upasana* only after he has attained *Sagunopasana*. Suddenly, it is impossible for one to get involved in *Nirgunobasana* straight away.

If we try to picturize the origin of this universe as stated in *Brahadaranyaka Upanishat* it will look as;

---

[1] *Brahmam is different from Brahma. Brahma is the chief of Devas. Brahmam is the top most one – Parabrahmam.*

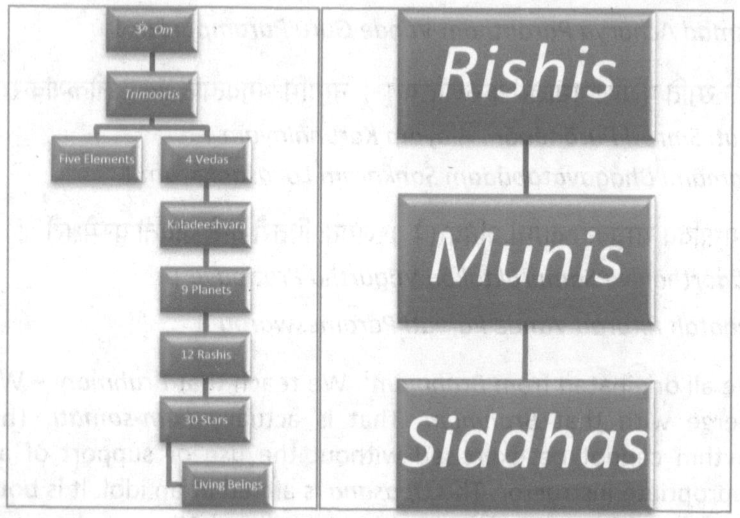

The *Aadhi Moolam*, also called as *Parabrahmam*, does not have any form or qualities. It does not fit within any limitations. However, in order to realize that *Brahmam* without any form, a sort of image worship is suggested. Once the maturity (*Saaloka*, *Saameepya* and *Saayujya*) is reached, there is no need for any restrictions and prescriptions to worship gods with different images, fasting, etc. Various *karmas* have to be performed to take us to that yogic position.

Shiva, *Shakti* and *Vishnu* are all one and the same. These three Gods are without origin. For all other Gods we could read the origin and for some we could read the end also in one or other *Purana* or stories.

In the form of *Arddhanaareeshwara* the left half of Lord *Shiva* is *Shakti*. Again, in the form of *Shankaranaaraayana*, the left half of Lord *Shiva* is *Vishnu*. This clearly implies that *Shakti* and *Vishnu* are the same and naturally *Shiva* also.

The 52nd name in Sri *Lalita Trishatee* is *Éśwarārdhānga Śarīrā* – one who has shared the half body with *Eeshwaran*.

In the same way, the 392nd name in Sri *Lalita Sahasranama* is *Śrīkaṇdārdhaśarīriṇī* – with the same meaning – one who has shared the half body with *Eeshwaran*.

Brahadaranyaka Upanishat verses (I–3, I–4), starting from *"Ātmaivetamagra Āseet"* till *"Sa Imamevātmānam Tvetāpātayat Tataḥ"* describes in this manner – the *Parabrahmam* seems to be two as husband and wife.

The energy of the *Parabrahmam* is *Sri Devi – Shakti*. Even when the power of that object is within it, the power cannot exist without the entity. Hence the *Parabrahmam* is the *Shakti* and the *Shakti* is the *Parabrahmam*. Both cannot be different.

In the same manner, if *Eshwaran* is considered as *Brahmam*, Goddess Ambikai is merged with that *Eshwaran*. Can the fragrant and the flower be separate? How about whiteness and the milk?

Ambikai is thus unsplittable from *Eeshvaran*. *Parameshwara* and *Paraashkati* are the earliest/ first couple to be inseparable; They are the mother and father of all living beings. Yet they are one and the same.

In *Sri Devi Maahaatmyam* (10-5) also *Sri Devi* herself affirms, "*Ekaivāham Jagat Yatra Dvitīyā Kā Mamāparā |*". I am the only one in this world. What or who else is there other than myself? When *Sri Devi* herself has told this, do we need any other assertion?

Chāndogya Upanishat (6:2:1) says "*Ekam Evātvetīyam*" – That is, all the Gods are same - there is only one God, no two. *Brahma Sootram* says "*Ekam Brahma Dvitīya Nāste Neha Naye Nāste Nāste Kinchana*" – there is only one God – no two – not at all two. *Yajur Veda* (32-3) utters – "*Na Tasya Pratimāsti Śutāma Pāpvitam*" – He is so holy and does not have any image.

Even in the daily *Panchaayatana* Puja only the images of the 5 Gods are not being used. Only something symbolically/ metamorphically is used.

The force of Parabrahmam, without any image, qualities and undefined, which includes a number of morphological, incomprehensible and inexhaustible materials, seems to be limited. The absolute philosophical paradigm is not amorphous.

However, we are not yet mature enough to realize the formless *Parabrahmam* (no need of writing/ reading this book, if we are that much mature). Someone has to hold back or attach side wheels until one learns to drive a bicycle. Once he becomes expert these are not needed. We need a boat to cross a river. Once we have reached the other shore, what is the need of a boat.

Therefore, until we are mature, we will try to learn about a God – why can't it be the holy mother - is it not that we get such a pleasure when we call mother as '*amma*'?

When we think of incarnation of God – immediately the 10 incarnations of Lord *Vishnu* (*dashaavatar*) only comes to our mind. If we think a little bit deep, one may be reminded of the 24 incarnations of Lord *Vishnu* as described in *Shrimad Vishnu Bhagavatam* (1.3.6-25).

However, the *Shakta* texts describe many an incarnation of *Sri Devi*, considered as sister of Lord *Vishnu*. It is attempted to understand some of such incarnations of *Sri Devi*. The related mantras are also indicated wherever possible.

In general, all the *mantras* are supposed to be secretive. All the more the *Shakti* related *mantras*. Hence, they are to be got initiated by an appropriate teacher (*guru*) only, before trying to chant of to do *japam*.

Can any Hindu religious book be written without quoting the speech of *Kanchi Paramaacharya* – that too about *Sri Devi* – impossible. Other religions have one single book as the base. But for our Hindu religion there are 1000s of books. In that case how anyone can understand from all these books? That is why we have one encyclopedia – called speeches of *Kanchi Paramaacharya*. Be it any subject and whenever and wherever needed we can always refer to his speeches. Can anyone wait for ghee when we have butter on hand? In that way his speeches have been referred in this book also in some places. To enjoy his speeches, they are given in his own words colloquially.

Generally, it is very difficult to read Samskruta words in English with proper pronunciation. It is apt to read them in Samskruta script itself. But to benefit those who cannot read Samskruta script the *mantras* have been given in English also. The Samskruta words, when transliterated in English are given in *italics*. Also, whenever She denotes Goddess *Sri Devi*, it is written as **She** or **Her**. Normally diacritical marks will be used for transliteration of Samskruta words into English. But general readers are not fully conversant with diacritical marks and hence they find it difficult to read. Hence, it not been used in this book in normal texts. But for proper pronunciation it has been completely used in *mantras*.

Humble pranāms are due to Pujyasri Pranavananda Swamiji of Ayyarmalai and Srisri Narahari Giri Swamijee, who have given his blessings and some pleasantries about the author and the book. They also have provided various inputs to this book.

Hearty thanks to all the good-hearted souls who enabled this book to be presented in this fashion. Attempts have been made to give this book as much error free as possible. Still if there are any errors, apologies are sought. If the errors are given as feedback, it will the next edition to be fault free.

There is no doubt that Sri Devi will shower her compassion and blessings to all those who read this book.

Chennai   *Dr. Ramamurthy N.*
2020

*****

Adi Shankara – Establisher of *Shanmatas*

Sri *Adi Shankara Bhagwat Pādar*, the greatest philosopher and thinker, in a short life span of 32 years, has created a collection of art-essays Indian culture and the intellectual and emotional integration of this sub-continent.

He called for the abolition of superstitions and practices and the supremacy of radical reasoning. The hard philosophies of the *Upanishats* were easily described by him for the benefit of those who were involved in unnecessary and useless verbal arguments.

Having traveled many times from east to west and south to North of India, he succeeded in convincing his opponents, not by sword or threats or charms, but by persuasive arguments about the teachings of the Vedas and especially the Upanishats. Such things can be achieved in such a short time only by an incarnation of the God. That is why, he is believed by of all the people of the world, to be the incarnation of the Supreme Being. He is the embodiment of the *Dakshinamoorti* manifestation and the supreme spiritual knowledge. The supreme beauty of his teaching is that it applies to all human beings irrespective of religion or race, caste or creed or nationality. That is the reason, he is aptly called as '*Jagadguru*' – teacher of the entire universe.

There is one name as "*Shanmada Stāpakar*" in the ashtotram of *Adi Shankarar* – the founder of *Shanmada*. He has sub-divided our religion of Hinduism, into six sub-religion kind of as;

1. *Gānapatyam* – People who primarily worship Lord *Ganapati*
2. *Shouram* – People who primarily worship Lord *Soorya*
3. *Shaivam* – People who primarily worship Lord *Shiva*
4. *Vaishnavam* – People who primarily worship Lord *Vishnu*
5. *Koumāram* – People who primarily worship Lord *Subramanya* (*Muruga or Kumara*)
6. *Shāktam* – People who primarily worship Goddess *Sri Devi* (*Shakti*)

Each of these *Shanmata* deities is found in various forms. Such variants differ in terms of image, clan, customs, patriotism and the need of the devotee. For instance;

* *Ganapati – Mahā Ganapati, Ucchishta Ganapati, Vallabha Ganapati, Siddhi Bhuddhi Ganapati, Ganapati* with two hands, *Ganapati* with five heads and so on.
* *Subrahmanyar – Muruga, Kumāra, Bāla Subrahmanyar, Subrahmanyar* with *Devasena, Subrahmanyar* with *Valli* and *Devasena* and so on.
* *Shiva – Rudra, Sarabeshwara, Bhairavar, Arddhanārīshwara, Shankara Narayana* and so on.
* *Vishnu – Ranganatha, Srinivasan, Rama, Krishna, Narasimha* and lot many names.
* *Shakti – Durga, Ashta Lakshmi, Sarasvati, Chāmundī, Dasha Maha Vidyas, Bhuvaneshwari, Tripurasundari, Shodashī, Maha Shodashī, Para Shodashī* and thousands of similar names.

Moreover, we cannot ignore the family deities, clan goddesses, Lord Iyyappa, Santoshi Mata, Kubera, etc. which do not fall within the above defined limits.

Although the worship of these deities had already been existing, Sri Adi Shankarar brought a system into play. These six religions are considered to be the branches of Hinduism. Later, the *Smārtas*, which is not one of the six branches, appear to be a branch of Hinduism, which in some sense is associated with *Shaivam*. In one perspective, they can be called *smārtas* because all the gods are worshipped in the same sense by them – *sama* + *artha*.

Even before *Sri Adi Shankara*, worshipping of these Gods were existing. *Sri Devi Bhagavatam* (7.39.30) reads as;

शिवाश्च वैष्णवाश्चैव सौरा: शाक्तास्तथैव च ।
गाणपत्या आगमाश्च प्रणीता: शङ्करेण तु ॥

Śivāśca Vaiṣṇavāścaiva Sourāḥ Śāktāstathaiva Ca |

Gānapatyaa Āgamāśca Praṇītāḥ Śankarena Tu ॥

To bring back those brahmins, who have gone against the path of *Vedas*, in the proper route, the auspicious scriptures like *Shaivam, Vaishnavam, Shakta, Souram* and *Gaanapatyam* were created properly. It may be worth noting that *Koumaaram* is not listed here.

Worshipping of these Gods were there even before *Sri Adi Shankara*. However, he only structured them and hence called as the author of *Shanmada* and Advaita doctrines. He also included one more sub-religion called *Koumaaram*. Hence the Advaita concepts are common to all the six sub-religions.

*****

Shāktam

There is nowhere else in the world where perfect love can be found, such as motherhood. Even if the child does not replicate his love, the mother has continued to make perfect love. Tamil proverb reads - "Mother's mind is manic, the child's is like a stone" - "பெற்ற மனம் பித்து, பிள்ளை மனம் கல்லு".

We can enjoy the perfect love and selfless labour only with a mother. When the child calls 'mother!', the pleasure of the mother is unique. This love is more enduring to the cow-clan than to the human race – the mother of the calf!

Let us enjoy *Paramacharya's* a little speech about *Ambikai*, possibly in his own words.

Our mother is the only for this body. After this birth then next birth – another mother. Destruction of the body does not kill *Atma*. There is only one mother for the *Atma*. *Sri Lalita Sahasranama* starts with *"Sri Mātre Namaḥ" Ambikai* is the *Jaganmata* – mother of this entire universe. All the energy we have is hers.

Continuously, the fragments of her energy are exhibited to all living organisms. Whatever we do, it is all hers. We cannot do anything. It is wrong to be arrogant thinking that we only did it.

Even if anything is not asked for, **she** will automatically grant them gimmicks, wealth, shine, etc., in the world and then bless them with the bliss also. When we have the supreme Advaita bliss, we become blissful. On the other hand, it is a condition that **she** will settle our *karma* and give liberation one day. Let it be available when it is available. We have a mother who loves us. It is now possible for us to remember her love and pray for her love. Is there anything more to enjoy? The entire world and all living beings will always be happy to think of the dear *Ambika* as a love.

Let us surrender the golden feet of the *Paramacharya*.

Shāktam - Worshipping *Sri Devi* as the primary Goddess. Among the *Shanmadas*, after *Shaivam* and *Vaishnavism*, the most popular god(dess) is *Shakti*. Even the followers of *Shiva*, have a practice of worshipping *Shakti*. *Navaratri* festival is meant for exclusively worshipping *Sri Devi*. *Shakti* worship is practiced and **she** is an important deity who is worshiped all-day, irrespective of religion, male, female and caste.

Ancient Tamil poetess Aouvaiyār also said "அன்னையும் பிதாவும் முன்னறித் தெய்வம் – Mother and father are the primary gods". She kept the mother first before even father. In the sequence "*Mata* (Mother), *Pita* (Father), *Guru* (teacher), *Deivam* (God)" also mother is given the top priority. Subramanya Bharathi also says, "ஆதிப் பரம் பொருளின் ஊக்கம் – அதை அன்னையெனப் பணிதல் ஆக்கம்". *Upanishat* also says "*Mātru Devo Bhava*". Thus, Mother is given importance in all places and father only secondary.

The thought of mother as a goddess, it is turned into – Goddess as mother - we worship "*Ambāl - Ambikai*". When *Paramātma* form is thought as a mother, more than any other form, the happiness overflows as bliss.

No matter how old are we, we become a baby to mother. We cling to absolute belief and surrender. To obtain the divine nature through the childish nature, we assume the *Paramātma* form into our mother. Hunger or any other desire we cling to the mother as '*amma*' – must hold her strongly.

If we presume *Paramātma* as a *Jagatjanani*, it is not that we enjoy something that does not exist. In fact, *Paramātma*, who is truly in love with all the qualities of the virtues, is the absolute motherhood. The *Paramātma* is everything, hence it blesses us in whatever form, we imagine. In the same way that *Parabrahmam* becomes a mother and with compassion, definitely it comes and satisfies our needs, when we pray, imagining it as a mother.

Why do we need a form when it is formless? We have a body, we are all born from that root, it is our mother, we are its children –

as long as we have this in mind, we need a form for the Parabrahmam also. When we have matured enough to understand that we do not have a form – we are all *Atma* only – once we have realized this, we do not need any form or shape for the *Parabrahmam*.

We do not need to pray to *Devi*, "you give me this or that". Doesn't the mother know what to give to us, based on our eligibility? However, this is not the case in practice. We have not yet got that prudence. We have been asking, "Please give me this – give me that and so on". That is why we do puja, *Upasana*, *japa*, etc. This is also not wrong. But this cannot be a permanent one. We need to get out of the worldly pleasures and move on to eternal bliss. We need to Pray to Mother God this maturity also.

Sri Devi is;

- *Nāyaki* as **she** is the consort of *Lord Shiva*
- *Nānmukkī* as **she** is the consort of *Lord Brahma* (four faced)
- *Nārāyanī* as **she** is the consort of *Lord Narayanan*
- *Shāmbhavī*, holding five flowers in hand, the world's greenest greenery.
- *Varāhi*, who destroys bad elements
- *Shoolini* holding a trident (*shoolam*)
- *Mātangī*, the daughter of sage *Matangar*

Thus, **she** is worshipped with different names, different forms, different actions, etc. However, it is the same *Shakti*, who creates, protects, destroys, covers and blesses this world – thus **she** plays. The entire universe originated from **her** and merges with **her** at the end. The name 'Uma' is same as the *Pranava Mantra* 'Om'. 'Hrīm' is the *Shakta Pranava Mantra*.

It is the unique feature of our Hindu religion to pray the God treating as a mother of all the creatures. The knowledge about the mother God is called *Sri Vidya*. The knowledge about the *Brahmam* is called *Brahma Vidya*. The sages used to say both *Srividya* and *Brahmavidya* are one and the same. The *Paramatma* signified by 'Om' in *Brahmavidya*, is signified by 'Hrīm' in *Sri*

Vidya. The root letter '*Hrīm* is called *Maya Bījam* (root letter) - *Bījam* means seed. The seed becomes a plant then becomes a *tree*. In the same manner the *Mahakali, Mahalakshmi* and *Mahasaraswati*, originate from this *Maya Bījam*.

The energy of the amorphous material is the female aspect. When the energy is formed, it becomes the mother. Swamy Vivekananda would say, "*Shakti* is the tidal wave in the calm waters of *Paramporul*". In the *Tantra Shastras*, the so-called *Shiva-Shakti* are respectively *Purusha-prakriti*, according to the Vedic system. In Advaita, they are called *Brahmam-Maya*. "By nature, both are the same. Every living thing is blissfully-sensitive" says Arthur Avalon.

The practice of worshipping god as a mother is not only in Hinduism but also in Vajrayana Buddhism and in Jainism.

The way of worshipping such *Ambika* is called *Srividya*. According to the *Srividya* practice of worship, it is very pleasing to Goddess *Sridevi*, if *Mahameru* or *Sri Chakra* Puja is performed.

Mahesha, Madhava, Vidhatru, Manmatha (Cupid), *Skanda, Nandi* (Bull God), *Indra, Manu, Chandra* (Moon), *Kubera, Agastya,* Lopamudra (wife of *Agastya*) and *Krota Bhattāraka* are the 12 major *Sri Vidya upasakas*. It is worth noting that Lord *Shiva* and *Vishnu* are also included in the list. They do not have any *gurus* (teachers). They only originated the method of worshipping *Sri Devi*.

The mother of all the *Yantras* or *Chakras* is the *Sri Chakra*. The word '*Sri*' is a symbol of greatness, passion and great prosperity.

Adi Shankarar, all over the Bharat that he visited, made everyone feel the pride of *Sri Chakra* and the cult of *Srividya*. Although seemingly he equally treated all the deities, he seems to have given importance to the worship of *Shakti*. He has gracefully authored commentary to *Sri Lalita Trishati* and also given us the noble beings of the *Soundaryalahari*.

*****

Shakta Texts

There are many texts related to *Shāktam*. Some of these are listed below. This is not a comprehensive list. Some of the important texts are recorded.

- *Tantra Rāja Tantrum*
- *Vāmakeshwara Tantrum* (part of *Nityā Shodashikārnavam*)
- *Kulārnavam*
- *Jnānārnavam*
- *Dattātreya Samhita*
- *Sharadha Tilakam*
- *Prapancha Sāram* (By *Adi Shankarar*)
- *Paramānanda Tantrum*
- *Chitkagana Candrika*
- *Panchāshtavam* (by *Kālidāsa*)
- *Shakti Mahimnā Stotram*
- *Lalita Stavaratnam* (By *Doorvāsa*)
- *Parashurāma Kalpa Sootram*
- *Tripurā Rahasyam*
- *Srividya Ratna Sutra-s* (By *Sri Gowdabādar*)
- *Soundaryalaharī* (By *Adi Shankarar*)
- *Sri Lalita Sahasranamam* and *Sri Lalita Trishatī* – mid of *Brahmānda Puranam*
- *Sri Devi Bhāgavatam*
- *Sri Devi Narayanīyam* – abridged form of *Sri Devi Bhagavatam* - By Pāleli Sri Narayana Namboothiri – with 41 *Dashakams* and 430 verses
- *Sri Devi Khadgamala Stotram* – amidst *Sri Vāmakeshwara Tantrum* as a dialogue between *Uma* and *Maheswaran*
- *Varivasya Rahasyam* (commentary for *Sri Lalita Sahasranamam* by *Sri Bhāskararāya*[2])
- *Gowrī Tantrum* amidst *Rudra Yāmalam*
- Commentary for *Sri Lalita Trishatī* by *Adi Shankarar*[3]
- *Kāmakalā Vilāsam*

---

[2] The author of this book has translated this commentary into English as a separate book.

[3] The author of this book has translated this commentary into English and Tamil as separate books.

- *Sri Vidya Tantrum*
- Lot many *Suktas* within *Rig Veda* like *Sri Suktam, Durga Suktam, Bhagya Suktam, Saraswathi Suktam, Sri Devi Suktam,* etc.
- *Sri Devi Bhāgavata Māhātmyam* amidst *Sri Skanda Puranam.*
- *Sri Devi Māhātmyam* amidst *Sri Mārkandeya Puranam.*
- Tantric Texts (around 22) by Sir John Woodroffe (Arthur Avalon)
- 33 *Shakta Upanishats* as listed below.

#	Veda	Upanishat
		Popular *Upanishats*
1.		*Bahvrochopanishat*
2.	*Rig Veda*	*Tripuropanishat*
3.		*Sowbhāgya Lakshmi Upanishat*
4.	*Krishna Yajur Veda*	*Saraswathi Rahasya Upanishat*
5.	*Sama Veda*	*Ārunikopanishat*
6.		*Arunopanishat*
7.		*Sitopanishat*
8.	*Atharva Veda*	*Sri Devi Atharva Shīrsham or Sri Devi Upanishat*
9.		*Annapoornopanishat*
10.		*Tripurā Tāpinīya Upanishat*
11.		*Bhāvanopanishat*
		Not so Popular *Upanishats*
12.		*Atharvashikopanishat*
13.		*Sri Chakra Upanishat*
14.		*Atharva Dvitīya Upanishat*
15.		*Alla Upanishat*
16.		*Kāmarāja Kīlidottāra Upanishat*
17.		*Gāyatri Upanishat*
18.	*Atharva Veda*	*Gāyatri Rahasya Upanishat*
19.		*Kālikā Upanishat*
20.		*Kālī Medādīkshita Upanishat*
21.		*Guhyakālī Upanishat*
22.		*Guhya Shodānyāsa Upanishat*
23.		*Tulasi Upanishat*
24.		*Pītāmbara Upanishat*

#	Veda	Upanishat
25.		*Muktikopanishat*
26.		*Rājashyāmalā Rahasya Upanishat*
27.		*Vanadurgā Upanishat*
28.		*Sāvitri Upanishat*
29.		*Sumukhya Upanishat*
30.		*Shyāma Upanishat*
31.		*Sri Vidyātāraka Upanishat*
32.		*Shodasha Upanishat*
33.		*Hamsashodasha Upanishat*

Though mantras for these Upanishats could be obtained with difficulty. The commentaries for some of them only could also be obtained. [4]

It is apparent, in many ways, that *Sri Adi Shankarar* gave great importance to *Shāktam*. Let us look at just a few examples. We may know by a handful the whole sack.

The writings of *Sri Adi Shankarar* include *Soundaryalaharī*, which is the epitome of the philosophy of the religion. It has 100 verses.

From the very words of Kanchi *Paramacharya* - *Sri Adi Shankarar* files an allegation on *Ambal* of stealing, in the 25th verse of his *Soundaryalahari;*

I mean - I close my eyes and try to meditate on you. I expected half male and half female body (*Ardhanārīshwara* form), because Lord *Parameshwara* has already given his half body to you. But you were seen in full female form – stealing the remaining half body also of Lord *Parameshwara* and seen in full female form.

As a young child, Thirugnana Sambandar started singing Thevāram "God with an ear ring" while singing the hymn of God.

---

[4] The author of this book has written and published books both in English and Tamil *"Shakta Upanishats"* giving the mantras of all the 33 *Upanishats* and commentaries for around 6 of them.

It was then itself, that he realized the Arddhanārīshwara form - the Siva-Shakti unified form.

Even in the very first verse of *Soundaryalaharī*, *Adi Shankara* says – It is only if the Lord *Mahadeva* is joined with you, the Supreme Being, he gets the power to make the universe. Otherwise he does not even be able to get the energy to move in the gutter. If that is the case with *Mahadeva*, how about deities like *Vishnu*, *Rudran*, *Brahma* and so on. Only with virtues of earlier births one can be able to worship you.

In the same way, in the 4th verse of *Soundaryalaharī*, he says – ordinarily Gods show the non-fearing and boon signets through their hands. But you display the signets through your legs in the dancing posture. Because your golden feet are the ones capable of saving the devotees from fear and giving them more than asked for.

Similar to *Soundaryalaharī*, *Sri Adi Shankara* has also written 100 verses on *Lord Shiva* called 'Sivānandalaharī'. *Sri Adi Shankara* has never praised Lord *Shiva* in his *Soundaryalaharī*. On the other hand, he talks about *Devi* in the very first verse of *Sivānandalaharī*. He says *pranāms* to Lord *Shiva* and his consort *Sri Devi*. Our Holy Mother (*Shivā*) is the repository of all knowledge, the arts, and the offers benefits of all. **She** is the offer of greatest blessings. **She** raises again and again in my heart and spreads highest happiness. Even when he wants to talk about the father, he could not forget mother.

In the same way, in the 61st verse of the same *Sivānandalaharī* he says – the minds of the devotees are attracted, becomes dependent, and merges together, towards the lotus feet of the *Sri Devi* alongwith *Pashupati*. He gives various comparisons in this regard – how the seeds of *Angola* tree are attracted back towards the tree – how a needle is attracted by a magnet – how a *Sumangala* lady is attracted towards her loving husband – how climbers are dependent on the trees – how the rivers merge themselves in the oceans.

In the 7th verse of *Devi Aparādha Kshamāpana Stotram* written by *Sri Adi Shankarar*, he says – only because he is wedded to you, he gets the role of *Jagadīshan* (Lord of this universe). Otherwise, he was just a watchman in a burial ground having the garland of skulls and the ashes throughout the body.

In this way, we can read 'n' number of examples. *Sri Adi Shankarar*, continues to compare Lord *Shiva* and *Sri Devi* – both wear the crescent moon on the crown. Both do not have origin neither end. Both are merged as two soul and a single body.

Kālidāsa, the greatest Samskruta poet declares, Lord *Shiva* and *Sri Devi* as the parent of the universe – he does not say that they are mother and father – but addresses with a single word 'Parent' – "*Jagata Pitarou*".

In our houses also, even though small children have a great respect towards their father, they do not take that much right as they take with their mother. In the same fashion, we, the children of our mother of universe take lots of rights with **her.** We cannot take comparatively that much rights with Lord *Shiva*.

Therefore, the elders have said that the *Shakta Upasana* is the transcendental device to attain liberation. We also feel it in many ways. Thus, let us all continue to worship *Sri Devi* and live a life of prosperity.

This in no way mean that worshipping the other deities is being belittled. *Shakta* worship is an easy tool for liberation (*moksha*). Further, all the gods are one and the same - only one. Whatever form of deity pleases him, let him worship that god and attain all kinds of attractions.

*****

Śrī Vidyā

In the first part of *Śrī Lalitā Trishatī*, it has been mentioned as "*Mokṣaika Hetu Vidyā Sā Śrī Vidyā Eva Na Samśayaḥ*". The only way to liberation (*moksha*) is *Śrī Vidyā*. There can be no doubt in this.

Lord *Parameswara* has blessed us all various *Vedas, Sastras, Smritis, Puranas, Itihāsas*, etc., to reach the eternal liberation. These depend on the devotee and his clarity of mind. *Śrī Ādhi Śaṅkarar* in his *Soundaryalaharī*, 31st verse, explains that *Parameswara*, after providing all the *Tantra Sastras* to this world, at the behest of *Śrī Devī*, blessed the world with *Śrī Tantra*, which is the gist of all the *Tantra Sastras*. This has got the special name called *Śrīpura Upāsanā or Śrī Vidyā*[5].

Worship (*Vidyā*) of *Devī*, who is denoted by the letter '*Śrī*' is *Śrī*

Vidyā[6]. The Samskruta letter '*Śrī*' has lots of meanings – particular meaning is wealth. In general, it means goddess *Lakshmi Devī*. Since everyone is behind money/ wealth, this worship is world famous. However, *Śrī Vidyā* is a path to worship Goddess *Durga*. *Śrī Vidyā* means knowledge of *Śrī Devī*, most important acquaintance or real path leading to liberation. This complicated, traditional worship will lead to adoration to various other Gods. *Śrī Chakra* or its highest form *Mahā Meru* is a representation of development in this regard.

---

[5] 585th name in *Śrī Lalitā Sahasranāma* is just *Śrī Vidyā*. It affirms that *Śrī Lalitā Devī* is *Śrī Vidyā* and *Śrī Vidyā* is *Śrī Lalitā Devī*.

[6] The author of this book has written a separate book called "Power of *Śrī Vidyā*"

The aim of the worship method called *Śrī Vidyā* is – realizing through experiences that self and *Parabrahmam* are one and the same – this is what the *Vedanta Maha* sentences communicate.

Kāñchi Paramācārya, who is considered as an incarnation of *Ādhi Śaṅkara*, has clearly explained in detail that *Brahma Vidyā* and *Śrī Vidyā* are one and the same (Voice of God volume 6). *Śrī Vidyā* is an ancient and most influential *Shakta tantra*. *Śrī Vidyā* can be majorly classified into three;

- Worshipping *Śrī Lalitā Tripurasundarī*
- **Her** *mantras*
- **Her** *yantra* called *Śrī Chakra*

Śrī Vidyā is composed of a systematic, orderly scheme that combines elements of perception, devotion and *yoga*. In the *Śrī Vidyā* tradition, *Śrī Chakram* is a *Yantra* (symbolic figure) for worship. When it is raised to a 3-dimensional figure, it becomes 'Meru'. Actually, the top angle view of *Meru* is the *Śrī Chakram*.

In *Śrī Chakram*, the journey from the exterior *Bhūpuram* till the central *Bindu* in a step by step path to one's own journey to reach the *Brahmam*. This ritual practice is known as the "*Navāvarṇa Puja*". *Āvarṇa* can mean a curtain, screen, block, fence, wall, fort, etc. However, in this context we can take it as enclosures located one by one. In fact, a devotee gradually crossing every *āvarṇa* and reaching/ connecting with the divine mother is, in practice, one by one removing the curtains of ignorance.

Each of the *āvarṇa* is dedicated to a particular God. There are Gods and hand signs (*Mudras*) pertaining to every stage of *Śrī Chakra*. When a devotee moves to next *āvarṇa* he is raised one step. The travel from the outer *Bhūpuram* till inner *Bindu* is, the awakening of man's dominant power – the *Kundalinī* energy sleeping in *Mūlādhāra* raises and surprisingly unifying with the *Brahmam* by reaching the *Sahasrāra*.

<u>Worshipping *Śrī Chakra*;</u>

It has been mentioned in the book called *"Lalitopākyānam"* as;

Kāmākśyeva Mahālakśmīḥ Chakram Śrī Chakrameva Ca |
Śrī Vidyaiva Parāvidyā…….. .

Only *Kamakshi* is *Mahalakshmi. Chakram* means it is *Śrī Chakram* and *Parāvidyā* is *Śrī Vidyā.* Worshipping of *Śrī Chakram* can be done as outward rituals (*Bahirmukha*[7]) in a common place like a temple for the welfare of the society as a whole. The procedures recommended in this regard are very laborious, but still a person can do it to the extent possible (*yatāśakti*). Or it can also be through inward rituals (*Antarmukha*[8]) in a house for the welfare of self and/ or the family. It is worshiped with its symbols through the *Mantras* and *Dyānas.*

The highest form of *Śrī Vidyā* is worshipping *Śrī Chakra* or *Meru* is

Navāvarṇa worship. Such a worship takes the devotee to Śrīpuram, by raising his subconscious carries itself to the body, self-recognition or illumination of the body. The devotee modifies his body itself as a place of worship. He burns it, by sacrificing the same, in the holy fire. By the grace of Lord *Śiva* and *Shakti* he gets back his body. He imagines himself as a female to worship the divine mother. The path travelled by the *Kundalinī* from *Mūlādhāra* till *Sahasrāra*, is

---

[7] 871st name in *Śrī Lalitā Sahasranāma – Bahirmukha Sudurlabhā –* बहिर्मुख सुदुर्लभा

[8] 870th name in *Śrī Lalitā Sahasranāma – Antarmukha Samārādhyā –* अंतर्मुख समाराध्या

the same the devotee travelling from *Bhūpuram* till *Bindu* in the *Navāvarṇa* worship, through the nine *āvarṇas*. It is similar to the unison of *Śiva* and *Shakti*. *Śiva* and *Shakti* are not different from *Parabrahmam*. It is there in the body of every human being. Our body is *Piṇḍāṇdam* and the universe is the *Aṇḍāṇdam*. Realizing that both *Piṇḍāṇdam* and the *Aṇḍāṇdam* are one and the same is *Advaitam* (no two).

Lastly, the celebrant's body itself, during worshipping, is assumed as an embodiment of a temple dwelled by *Śrī Devī* herself. This is the highest maturity stage of *Śrī Vidyā*. Any ritual done, without understanding the inherent philosophies is a wasteful exercise. It has been compared to a donkey loaded with the sandal woods does not know the significance of sandal – neither know the difference between a thorn wood and a sandal wood. It is the fate of the donkey. Same way it is the fate of the worshipper. Hence it is imperative, for the worshipper to comprehend the inherent importance behind the traditional rituals and then follow the same. Then only he gets the complete benefit of them. *Śrī Chakra* worship is a spectacular tool of this universe, for stimulating our mind and spiritually develop self and our ancient *sanātana dharma*. Hence, the *Pancadaśākṣarī* and *Ṣoḍaśākṣarī mantras* are initiated only to those disciples, who completely surrender with the *guru*.

<u>The worship and the worshipper</u>

Those who worship *Shakti* are called *Shaktas*. Those who do *Śrī Vidyā* pooja are called *Upāsakas*. *Mantra*, *yantra* and *tantra* are the three vertices of the *Śrī Vidyā* triangle. The *mantra* is displayed in the *yantra*. The inward or outward *pooja* in a *yantra* is practically depend on the performance of performer and his capacity. The main *mantra* of *Śrī Vidyā* is the *Pancadaśākṣarī*. The main *yantra* of *Śrī Vidyā* is the *Śrī Chakra*. The key part of it is that *Śrī Devī* herself is iconized in the *tantra*, *mantra* and *yantras*. The *Śrī Vidyā* worship has to be performed with focused mind, appreciation and kindness in the heart. In that case, the *mantras*, *yantras*, offering, the pooja process and the disciplines are all converted into the expressions of *Chit-Shakti* form. The inherent philosophy is to transform the contents and the ordinary experiences into the bliss of the divine mother.

Soudaryalaharī affirms – If someone is subtly committed to heart and perform the worship – his ordinary speech becomes *japam*, the normal work of his hands becomes signets, his general walking becomes circum-ambulation (*pradakśinam*), taking food is offering in a holy fire and normal lying down becomes bowing. That is, what the person naturally does is converted into a worship. He need not separately do anything.

Only a male or a couple (husband and wife) are eligible to do most of the *karmas* prescribed in *Vedas*. But, *Śrī Vidyā* is an exception. It can be followed by any one at any time – irrespective of caste, creed, sex, etc. *Śrī Krishna* himself says in *Gīta* (9-32);

> *"Striyo vaiśyāḥ tatā sūdrāḥ tespi yānti parām gatim|"*

However, some rules like dos and don'ts are prescribed for the worshippers of *Śrī Vidyā*.

> *"Na Śaḍāya Na Duṣṭāya Nā Viṣvāsāya Garhicit |"*

The *gurus* have been cautioned by *Sastras*, not to initiated, immoral persons, characterless (blackguards) persons and those who do not have confidence on *Śrī Vidyā*.

It has been mentioned that the *upāsakas* of *Śrī Vidyā* have to follow some rules. The worshipper should;

- Not talk ill or wrong of other *Upasana* methods
- Always do *japa* in the background.
- Not demand offerings neither accept from others.
- Continue to do his duties properly
- Worship God, without expecting any fruits.
- Be fearless
- Not accept wealth and money with a selfish intention.
- Should not consider anything above than self-realization

- Importantly should not be revealing that he is *Śrī Vidyā upāsaka*. *Śrī Vidyā Upasana* is very secretive and the secrecy should always be maintained.

Stages of <u>*Śrī Vidyā*</u> – There are many steps in the ladder of *Śrī Vidyā*;

- Frist stage – *Mahā Gaṇapati Upasana* – in the *Śrī Vidyā* tradition *Gaṇapati* is called as "*Śrī Vidyā Mahā Vallabha Gaṇapati*". This is to get rid of all the obstrucles.
- Next is *Mahā Śyāmalā* called as *Mantrinī upāsana*. This is to get good intelligence. This *mahā mantra* has 98 letters. A book called "*Matanga Manukoṣam*" says that once this mantra is obtained, all other mantras can be got, just by going through once.
- Next in the sequence in *Vārāhi upāsana* – a person who is successful in his life should realize that the basis for the entire cosmos. Getting that cosmic consciousness is the goal of *Vārāhi upāsana*.
- Next is an important stage in *Śrī Vidyā* – *Bālā upāsana* – *Tripura Rahasya* says "*Bālā Līlā Viśiṣtatvād Bāleti Gatitāpriye*". *Paradevata* loves to play like a little girl and hence this name. This mantra is also called as *Laghu Śrī Vidyā mantra*. The word *Laghu* in Samskrutam has two meanings – easy and brief. Both the senses befit here.

- The three lettered (*Trayakṣara*[9]) mantra of *Bālā Tripura Sundarī* gets expanded to the next stage called *Mahā Pañcadaśākṣarī mantra*
- And to the next stage *Śrī Ṣoḍaśākṣarī mantra*.

---

[9] 630th name in *Śrī Lalitā Sahasranāma – Trayakṣarī –* त्रयक्षरी

Two different paths are there in *Śrī Vidyā upāsana* – *Koula mārga* and *Samaya mārga*. *Samaya mārga* again has two variations – *Dakśiṇācāra* and *Vāmācāra*. Each of these two various has three sub-sections called *Bāhyā* (*Aparā*), *Āndra* (*Parā*) and *Parāparā* (both mixed).

Śrī Vidyā						
Samaya mārga [10]						Koula mārga [11]
Dakśiṇācāra			Vāmācāra			
Bāhyā	Āndra	Parāparā	Bāhyā	Āndra	Parāparā	

Clearly understanding *Śrī Vidyā upāsana* in the above routes/ stages will lead to satisfaction and fulfilment for the different and sometimes contradicting minds of the human beings.

A well-known great person Ramakrishna Paramahamsa authoritatively confirms – one real *Śrī Vidyā upāsakar* can only be real *Śāktar*. He can also be *Śaivite* outside, *Vaiṣṇavaite* in practice. Such a reconciliation is possible. He has proved that all the paths, once followed with devotion leads to the same single God. The *mantras* are definitely rewarding. *Yantras* are surely powerful. There are definitely gods and high powers. *Siddhis* can be achieved. The benefit of worship of the divine mother, gradually elevates in the right path till the goal is reached.

Tantras say – following the *Śrī Vidyā upāsana* without mental maturity or without proper guidance from an appropriate *guru*, is like walking on the edge of a sword. It is like hugging the neck of a tiger – like hanging a snake in the neck. Such a danger may happen.

Śrī Vidyā is not something, which everyone can get. This is the only path/ tool to liberation. For whomsoever, this is the last birth or who is in the form Śaṅkara he only will be fortunate to get initiated in *Śrī Vidyā*.

---

[10] 98th name in *Śrī Lalitā Sahasranāma* – *Samayācāratatparā* – समयाचारतत्परा
[11] 441st name in *Śrī Lalitā Sahasranāma* – *Koulamārgatatparasevitā* – कौलमार्गतत्परसेविता

Mantra Upāsana

Any God can be worshipped in *Moorthy* (image), *Yantra* and *Mantra* forms. The appropriate methods of adoring are explained in detail in our *Shastra* texts.

Out of these, the *Moorthy* is the image as a drawing or stone or metal sculpture – the physical form of the God alongwith all the organs and qualities, as described in the *Dhyana shloka* of that particular God. *Mantra* is the sound form of the God. The *yantra* is the subtle (*Sookshuma*) form of the God, whom we worship, without qualities.

Yantra is in between with form and formless. Gods are there in the *yantras*, but not in the form with organs and all.

"Yantram Mantramayam Proktā Mantrātmā Devederitā"

Yantra is the same as *mantra* – *mantra* is the God. There is no difference between the three types. The below names from *Sri Lalita Sahasranama* indicate that Sri Devi is in the form of mantras;

- 88ᵗʰ name – *Mūlamantrātmikā*
- 204ᵗʰ name – *Sarvamantra Svarūpiṇī*
- 846ᵗʰ name – *Mantrasarā*

Again, the below names, *Sri Devi* is in the form of the 3 *kootas* of *Panchadashaasharee*, the *maha mantra*;

- 85ᵗʰ – *Śrīmad Vāgbhava Kūṭaika Swaroopa Mukapankajā* – *Vāgbhava Kūṭa* the facial region of *Sri Devi*.
- 86ᵗʰ – *Kanṭhādha Kaṭiparyanta Madhya Kūṭa Svarūpiṇī* – *Madhya Kūṭa* the region from neck to hip of *Sri Devi*.
- 87ᵗʰ – *Śaktikūṭaika Tāpanna Katyadho Bhāgadhāriṇī* – the third *Śakti Kūṭa* the region below the hip of *Sri Devi*.

From this it is very clear that there is no difference between the form described by the *mantras* and the physical form of *Sri Devi*. We are all aware that *Sri Lalita Trishatee* gives 300 divines of the holy mother. All these 300 names are derived from the 15 letters of the *Panchadashaasharee maha mantra* @ 20 names for each letter totaling 15 x 20 These 300 names are divided into three groups viz. *Vāgbhava Kūṭa*, *Madhya Kūṭa* and *Śakti Kūṭa* each having 100 + 120 + 80 names respectively. Each can be construed as a *mantra* rather than name.

"Mantrāṇām Achintya Śaktidā" – the power of the *mantras* cannot be obtained by anyone. There is no difference between the *mantras* we chant and the relevant deity. The most important step in the *Upasana* is the solid belief that the both are one and the same.

Shastras say *"Saptakoti Mahā Mantrāḥ Śiva Vaktrāt Vinirgatāḥ"* – there are 7 crores of *mantras*. Wherefrom they all originated? The *Dhyana* verse of *Shrimad Bhagavad Gita* declares – *"Dyānāvastita Tadgatena Manasā Pashyanti Yam Yoginaḥ"* – that is, when the sages were in deep meditation these *mantras* emanated to their mind as intuition. That is the reason the sages are called *Mantra-Draṣṭā*.

In the last century also, *Sri Sri Bharathi Teertha Maharaj Swamiji* (head of *Puri Shankara Mutt*), did penance in the forests of Sringeri (1917-19). At that time the 16 *mantras* – each one line came to his mind and he formulated them as formulae as "Vedic Mathematics[12]". He himself mentioned this in the preface of his book. Though they are all single line formulae any type of mathematical problem can be resolved using one or more of these formulae. Also, this is called Mental Mathematics.

<u>Types of Mantras</u>

The text called *Sharada Tilaka* divides the mantras, fundamentally into 3 types – Masculine, Feminine and Neutral (*Napumsaka*);

---

[12] The author of this book has written a book on "Vedic Mathematics" explaining all the 16 formulae + 14 corollaries.

"Pumstrī Napumsakātmanoḥ Mantrā Sarve Samīritāḥ"

Further, depending on the number of letters in the mantras, they are divided into as below, by the text called *"Mantra Mahodadi"*;

- *Mantras* containing only one letter are called '*Piṇḍam*'
- *Mantras* containing two letters are called '*Kartrī*'
- *Mantras* containing three to nine letters are called '*Bījam*'
- *Mantras* containing ten to twenty letters are called '*Mantram*'
- *Mantras* containing more than twenty letters are called *"Mālā Mantram"*

The mantras befitting for self should be got initiated by an appropriate *guru*, what is called as *Upadesa Deeksha*. *"Dīkṣā Janma Tritīyakam"* – obtaining such *Upadesa Deeksha* is like a third birth[13] for the *upasaka*.

Sri Vidya Mantras

We are all aware that '*Om*' is the universal *Pranava Mantra* and '*Hrīm*' is the *Shakta Pranava Mantra*. The letter *Hreem* has a significant place in the *Shakta Upasana*. It is also called a single letter *mantra* and *Shakti Beejaaksharam* as well.

There are various *mantras* relating to *Sri Devi*. Some of them are listed below in groups. Only the name of the *mantra* is indicated – the *mantra* per se is not provided. Anyone who wants to know the *mantra* can approach an appropriate teacher.

- *Śrī Mahā Kāli Mantrāḥ*
    - *Śrī Navākṣarī Mantraḥ*
    - *Śrī Mūladurgā Mantraḥ*
    - *Śrī Durga Dvādaśākṣarī Mantraḥ*
    - *Śrī Mahiśa Mardinī Mantraḥ*
    - *Śrī Shūlinī Durgā Mantraḥ*
    - *Śrī Dīpa Durgā Mantraḥ*

---

[13] First birth is from the mother and second is getting *Upanayana*

- o *Śrī Vana Durgā Mantraḥ*
- o *Śrī Druṣṭi Durgā Mantraḥ*
- o *Śrī Swayamvara Durgā Mantraḥ*
- o *Śrī Jaya Durgā Mantraḥ*
- *Śrī Mahā Lakśmī Mantrāḥ*
  - o *Śrī Lakśmī Dvādaśākśara Mantraḥ*
  - o *Śrī Lakśmī Trayovimśadyakśara Mantraḥ*
  - o *Śrī Kamala Vāsinī Mantraḥ*
  - o *Śrī Kamala Lakśmī Mantraḥ*
  - o *Śrī Siddha Lakśmī Ekādaśākśara Mantraḥ*
  - o *Śrī Dana Lakśmī Mantraḥ*
  - o *Śrī Sowbhāgya Lakśmī Mantraḥ*
  - o *Śrī Vasudā Lakśmī Mantraḥ*
- *Śrī Mahā Saraswatī Mantrāḥ*
  - o *Śrī Saraswatī Daśākśara Mantraḥ*
  - o *Śrī Saraswatī Ekādaśākśara Mantraḥ*
  - o *Śrī Dhāraṇa Saraswatī Mantraḥ*
  - o *Śrī Chintāmaṇi Saraswatī Mantraḥ*
  - o *Śrī Nakulī Saraswatī Mantraḥ*
  - o *Śrī Nīla Saraswatī Mantraḥ*
  - o *Śrī Saraswatī Navākśarī Mantraḥ*
  - o *Śrī Mūkāmbikā Mantraḥ*
  - o *Śrī Hamsa Vāgīśwarī Mantraḥ*
  - o *Śrī Vāṇī Saraswatī Mantraḥ*
- *Śrī Daśa Mahā Vidyā Mantrāḥ* [14]
  - o *Śrī Dakśiṇa Kāli Mantraḥ*
  - o *Śrī Tārā Mantraḥ*
  - o *Śrī Ṣoḍaśī Mantraḥ*
  - o *Śrī Bhuvaneśwarī Mantraḥ*
  - o *Śrī Tripura Bhiravī Mantraḥ*
  - o *Śrī Chinna Mastā Mantraḥ*
  - o *Śrī Dhūmāvatī Mantraḥ*
  - o *Śrī Bhagalāmukkī Mantraḥ*
  - o *Śrī Rāja Mātangī Mantraḥ*
  - o *Śrī Kamalātmikā Mantraḥ*

---

[14] * These Devis have been discussed in some other chapter with a little more detail.

The author of this book has written separate books on *"Daśa Mahā Vidyā* Devis and Navavarna Devis.

- *Śrī Mahā Vidyā Mahā Mantrāḥ*
  - *Śrī Bhuvaneśwarī Ekākśara Mantrāḥ*
  - *Vāg Śrīpuṭita Trayakśara Bhuvaneśwarī Mantrāḥ*
  - *Pāśānguśa Puṭita Trayakśara Bhuvaneśwarī Mantrāḥ*
  - *Vāgbhava Bīja Puṭita Trayakśara Bhuvaneśwarī Mantrāḥ*
  - *Śrī Bhuvaneśwarī Chaturakśara Mantrāḥ*
  - *Śrī Bhuvanāmbā Mālā Mantrāḥ*
- *Śrī Vidyā Mahā Mantrāḥ*
  - *Śrī Vidyā Parameśwarī Angabhūta Śrī Rāja Mātangī Mahā Mantraḥ*
  - *Śrī Mātangī Angabhūta Śrī Laghuśyāma Mantraḥ*
  - *Śrī Mātangī Upāngabhūta Śrī Vāgvādinī Mantraḥ*
  - *Śrī Mātangī Pratyanga Devatā Śrī Nakulī Vāgīśwarī Laghuśyāma Mantraḥ*
  - *Śrī Vidyā Parameśwarī Angabhūtā Śrī Mahā Vārāhī Mantraḥ*
  - *Śrī Mahā Vārāhī Angabhūtā Śrī Laghu Vārtālī Mantraḥ*
  - *Śrī Mahā Vārāhī Upāngabhūta Śrī Swapna Vārāhī Mantraḥ*
  - *Śrī Mahā Vārāhī Pratyanga Devatā Śrī Traskariṇī Mantraḥ*
  - *Śrī Vidyā Parameśwarī Angabhūta Śrī Bālā Parameśwarī Mantraḥ*
  - *Śrī Bālā Parameśwarī Upāngabhūta Śrī Annapūrṇā Mantraḥ*
  - *Śrī Vidyā Parameśwarī Pratyangabhūta Śrī Aṣvārūḍā Mantraḥ*
- *Śrī Titi Nityā Mahā Mantrāḥ*
  - *Śrī Kāmeśwarī Nityā Mantraḥ*
  - *Śrī Bhagamālinī Nityā Mantraḥ*
  - *Śrī Nityaklinnā Nityā Mantraḥ*
  - *Śrī Beruṇḍā Nityā Mantraḥ*
  - *Śrī Vahni Vāsinī Nityā Mantraḥ*
  - *Śrī Mahā Vajreśwarī Nityā Mantraḥ*
  - *Śrī Śivadhūtī Nityā Mantraḥ*
  - *Śrī Tvaritā Nityā Mantraḥ*
  - *Śrī Kulasundarī Nityā Mantraḥ*
  - *Śrī Nityā Nityā Mantraḥ*
  - *Śrī Nīlapatākā Nityā Mantraḥ*
  - *Śrī Vijayā Nityā Mantraḥ*

- o *Śrī Sarva Mangalā Nityā Mantraḥ*
- o *Śrī Jvālāmālinī Nityā Mantraḥ*
- o *Śrī Chitrā Nityā Mantraḥ*
- *Śrī Chakra Navāvarṇa Devatā Mahā Mantrāḥ*
  - o *Śrī Pratama Āvarṇa Mantraḥ*
  - o *Śrī Dvitīya Āvarṇa Mantraḥ*
  - o *Śrī Triitīya Āvarṇa Mantraḥ*
  - o *Śrī Turīya Āvarṇa Mantraḥ*
  - o *Śrī Panchama Āvarṇa Mantraḥ*
  - o *Śrī Śaṣṭa Āvarṇa Mantraḥ*
  - o *Śrī Saptama Āvarṇa Mantraḥ*
  - o *Śrī Aṣṭama Āvarṇa Mantraḥ*
  - o *Śrī Navama Āvarṇa Mantraḥ*
- *Other Devatā Mantrāḥ*
  - o *Śrī Gowrī Panchākśarī Mantraḥ*
  - o *Śrī Dharaṇī Mantraḥ*
  - o *Śrī Hiraṇyeśwarī Mantraḥ*
  - o *Śrī Indrāṇī Mantraḥ*
  - o *Śrī Māyā Mantraḥ*
  - o *Śrī Pulindinī Mantraḥ*
  - o *Śrī Renukā Mantraḥ*
  - o *Śrī Śītalā Mantraḥ*
  - o *Śrī Vajra Prastāriṇī Mantraḥ*

Most of the *Devis*, whose *mantras* are mentioned above, have been discussed in different chapters next.

Results of chanting *mantras*

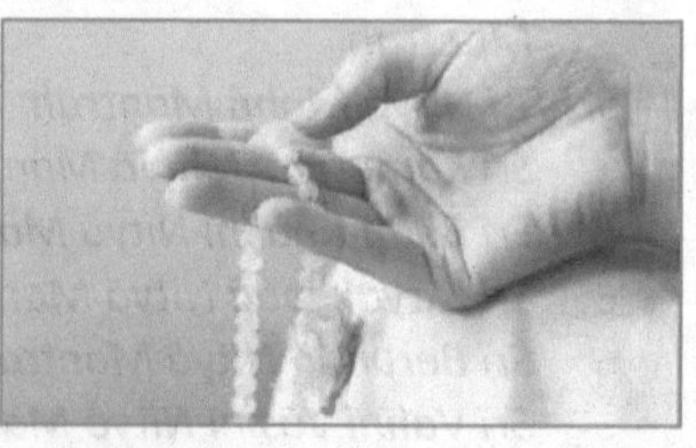

Mantras and *Upasanas* are very effective. We have all been hearing the best possible outcomes. There are various great benefits mentioned for each of the *mantras*. Several people have experienced it many times. However, some people claim that their rituals or the chanting of the *mantras* were fruitless. They say that the *mantras* do not have the power. Actually, that is not the case. Nay.

If the results mentioned were read with close attention – one has to perform the Upasana/ Puja/ Japa, with devotion. It is not ordinary devotion – there is also an adjective. "*Ananya* (without any other thought – with concentration – with focus mind – not monotonous)" – with love and leak tears. As Bhagavan Sri Krishna said in Gita - "*Ananyā Chintayanto Mām Ye Janā Paryupāsate*".

Now if everybody thinks – do we think of the deity without any other thought while chanting japa? Does the mind think of the deity alone and chant the mantras or perform puja? The fault lies on us. The *mantras* are definitely with the same power. They are worthy of more and more benefits. It is only for the preachers to take advantage of them. Even so, the deities, in particular Mother God, are waiting for us with her generous grace. **She** will continue to bless us. If we perform puja and all with more devotion – **she** is waiting for her blessings. It is for us to exploit these *mantras* and pujas.

Just to stress this point even at the cost of duplication, it has been repeated. All *mantras* should be obtained by a Guru before starting to chant. The books (including this book) should not be used to learn the *mantras*. They are mentioned in books for reference and understanding. After getting initiated by the *Guru*, the mantras, possibly with meanings, should be well understood and retained in the mind. Definitely all the benefits can be gained by praying with the *Devata* in mind.

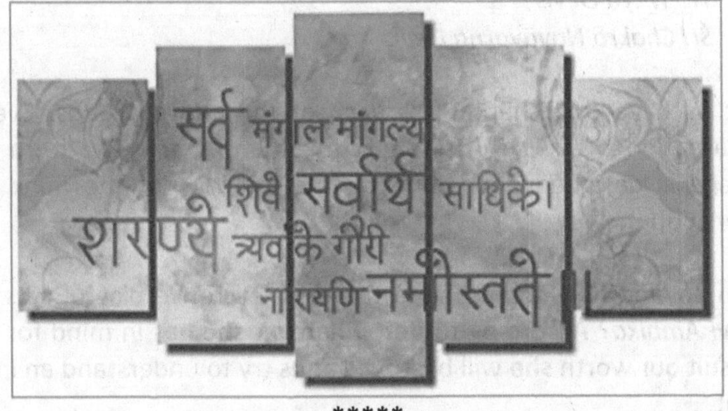

*****

Incarnations of *Śrī Devī*

We have plenty of names about *Sri Devi* – as *archanas* in the format of *Sahasranama, Trishatee, Ashtotra* and so on. All those different names cannot be construed as diverse incarnations. *Sri Devi* with the same image or form is addressed with various names.

If we try to define incarnation – first it should have different-different forms or images. Each of such image should have a purpose or role to play. This book intends only to address such different incarnations of *Sri Devi*.

The playful acts **she** made in each incarnation were many. No one can know about all the acts of **her** in all the *avatars* in full. We have tried to give this book as much as **she** wants to think about **her**. Isn't everything **her** act – her power? By her grace we bow her lotus feet.

The avatars of the Ambika can be classified into the following groups;

- *Śrī Vidyā Devis*
- *Chaṇḍī* – Three Great *Devis*
- *Saptaśatī* Chapter *Devis*
- *Daśa Mahā Vidyā Devis*
- Seven Mothers
- *Titi Nityā Devis*
- *Śrī Chakra Navāvarṇa Devis*

Let us have one chapter for each of the above groups. Every incarnation of *Sri Devi* is the form of *Brahmam*. The form or image is designed depending on the maturity of the mind of worshipper.

Can anyone fully comprehend the most secretive playful acts of *Devi Ambika*? According to **her**, whatever **she** has in mind for us to suit our worth **she** will bestow. Let us try to understand an iota of it.

Just thinking of **her** will fetch us everything we ask for. Why should we ask? Mother doesn't know what the child wants? Does not the mother in our house, feed the baby before even he cries? It is doubtless that our *Jagan Matha Ambika* will give us whatever reasonable we want.

Nobody knows about all the incarnations of Sri Devi. Even the great *yogis* and the *sadhus* could not know her at all fully. The great Sage Agastya, prayed to his Guru Hayagriva and begged by catching his feet and learned Sri Lalita Sahasranama and Sri Lalita Trishatee. If that is fate for person like him – how about us! We have got an opportunity to think of something about her. Let us try.

*****

Śrī Vidyā Devis

It was mentioned earlier that there are different steps/ stages in *Sri Vidya Upasana*. Let us try to understand something more in detail.

Bālā

The first known form *Srividya* is the juvenile form *Śrī Rājarājeśwarī* as *Bālā*. This has been clearly ascertained by *Purānās* like *Brahmānda*. In *Śrī Lalitā Sahasranāma* also *Śrīdevī* has been praised as *Bālāvikramananditā* (74th name) and *Bālālīlāvinodinī* (966th name). After destructing *Bhandāsurā* alongwith his aide demons and his huge army, *Bālā* returned from the battle with pride – says history.

It was mentioned that the *Bālā mantra* is foremost in *Srividyaā*. This *mantra* has three *Bījākśaras* (root letters) *Bīja* means seed. The seed when sowed takes the help of the Earth, air, water, light, etc., grows as a very big tree. Similarly, the three *Bījākśaras* of *Bālā mantra* matures as *Mahā Ṣodaśī* and *Parā Ṣodaśī* and blesses emancipation and liberation (*jīvan Mukti* and *Videha Mukti*) to her devotees. The three *Bījākśaras* of *Bālā mantra* are called as *Vāgbhava bīja*, *Kāmarāja bīja* and *Shakti bīja*, as discussed in the earlier chapter. When these *bīja*-s are adored the worshipers will be blessed with a communication skill – to effectively converse what he thinks in his mind to attractively reach others. *Bālā Tripurasundarī* is the one who can bless this art.

In the same way the second *Bīja* is *Kāmarāja Bīja*. In Samskrutam, *Bīja* means desire. There are two methods to satisfy the desires of human being. One is to satisfy him by satiating his wishes. The other one is – admitting him as a devotee by destroying his desires. Even if God gives everything he wants, sometimes it may backfire and ruin himself. For instance, if a child wants to play with a knife, the elders will not allow this. It is not that the elders do not want the child to play, but the knife may hurt him. Hence his mother hides the knife and diverts him to something of interest. Similarly, *Bālā* also evaluates every desire of each devotee and decides whether to provide the wish or not. If **she** feels that it would be against him, then she diverts his mind and blesses him with what is suitable for him and what is he worthy off. Probably the diverting the mind of a baby is easier for a mother than diverting the mind of an elderly person by *Bālā*. This way the entire world gets peace of mind and welfare.

The second method – the happiness obtained will be multifold than that obtained from getting the desired object. The desire of getting something itself is eradicated. For instance, if a person is in need of ₹ 10,000 and when he gets ₹ 1,00,000 then the earlier desire of ₹ 10,000 itself is no more a desire for him. In the same fashion, *Śrīdevī* showers everything on a devotee and eradicates the desires on this world itself. This is the greatest method ever.

The last *Bījākṣara* is *Śakti bīja*. An important energy for a human being is the physical energy or strength. But this alone is not adequate. During aged days this will be much reduced leading to lot of illness. Hence the mental power or will power be a higher form of energy. One can get anything and everything with this. When this mental energy is reduced the entire life is spoiled. Hence *Bālātripurasundarī* blesses her devotees with this energy and protects them. Hence this *mantra* is called *Rakṣarī* (the protecting one) *mantra*. When this mantra is initiated with six letters (*Ṣodaśī*) this *mantra* energy resides in the depth of the minds of the devotees and renders lots of great benefits. *Paraśurāma Kalpa Sūtra* insists that this *mantra* has to be taught only for those who are properly initiated by an appropriated *Guru* (teacher). That great is this *Bālā Vidyā*. This has to be got initiated through an appropriate *guru* either as *upadeśam* or as *dīkṣā* and has to be strictly/ religiously followed without any break.

Though this *Bālā Vidyā* is part of *Pancadaśī* and *Ṣodaśī Vidyā*-s there is a practice that this alone can also be worshipped as a main one. Hence, as *Navāvarṇa pūja* is done, *Bālā-āvarṇa pūja* method is also prescribed in many *tantras* to worship *Śrīdevī*.

Among the three forms viz. *Stūla* (physical), *Sūkśma* (subtle) and *Parā* (external), the last one is considered as the greatest by all. The *sūkśma* form is the *Bālā mantra*. However, it is very difficult for all to understand and worship in these forms. Hence the *tantra*-s have also prescribed the *Stūla* form. The *dyāna* (meditation) verse says that in this form *Śrīdevī* has *Japamālā* (garland of beads), book, *abhaya* and *varada mudras* (gestures of fearlessness and generosity) in all her four hands. **She** sits in *padmāsana* posture on a lily flower.

It is very easy to practice this *Bālā Vidyā* than any other *Vidyā*-s. This removes all the hurdles till one attains liberation. To obtain the compassion of this *Bālātripurasundarī*, one has to understand this *Vidyā* from learned and who regularly practice this *Vidyā*. If so, there is no doubt that the devotee will get kind grace of *Bālā*.

Bhuvaneśwarī

Śrīdevī in her *stiti* status praised as, *Rājarājeśvarī*, *Bhuvaneśvarī*, *Mahārājne* and so-on. On the whole there are 14 worlds (*loka*-s). They are − the earth (*Bhū loka*). Six worlds above this viz. - *Bhuvar, Suvar, Mahar, Jana, Tapa* and *Satya loka*-s. There are seven worlds beneath the Earth viz. - *Atala, Vitala, Sutala, Talātala, Mahātala, Rasātala* and *Pātāla loka*-s. These are called 14 *loka*-s or worlds. *Śrī Bhuvaneśvarī* unites all these 14 worlds within **herself** and rules them efficiently. **She** is the goddess, who protects all the living beings in all these worlds by providing

whatever necessary for each one of them and takes them along the *Ātma Mārg*.

It is **her** compassion that protects these worlds like a hen protects the egg. **She** not only protects the human beings but also all living things right from a worm onwards, based on the rewards of *Karma* of each one. Hence the name *Lokanāyakī* is very much apt for **her**. In *Śrī Lalitā Sahasranāma* also **she** is most befittingly called as *Ābrahmakīṭajananī* - आब्रह्मकीटजननी (285th name) – which means that **she** is the mother of all right from *Brahma* onwards till a worm.

The *bījākṣara* of this *Bhuvaneśvarī Devī* is a single letter *'Hrīm'*. This is a very powerful *bīja*. This is also called as *Śākta Praṇava mantra*. Out of the 300 names in *Śrī Lalitā Triśatī* 60 names start with the letter *'Hrīm'*. In that case, the glory of the letter needs any more stress? In *Bṛhadārāṇya Upanishat*, while describing the mind and the status of the mind, the *tattva* (philosophy) called *'Hrīm'* has been mentioned.

This *bījā Hrīm* is a combination of the letters *'ha'*, *'ra'* and *'ī'* suffixed by the *anusvāram*. This *bījā* is very secret and has to be advised or initiated by an appropriate *Guru*. The devotees, who regularly chant this mantra, as prescribed, will get every facility in his life till he gets liberation. There is not even an iota of doubt in this. His devotion will grow. He gets the knowledge of *Vedanta* and all. He will get everything taught from the *Guru* and attain emancipation.

The letter *'ha'* in this indicates the *prakāśa tattva*. Next letter *'ra'* indicates *vimarśa* status. Absolving all these 14 worlds within and creating the deluge is explained with this. Presenting these two statuses is the next letter *'ī'*. This *Bhuvaneśvarī* mantra indicates the action of creating the 14 worlds and then absolving them self within. The last *anusvāram* indicates the 5 tasks of *Śrī Devī*. The 5 tasks being:

1. Creation – creating the world and all living beings.
2. Protection – safeguarding the living beings.
3. Destruction (*layam*) – creating the entire world afresh after absolving the living beings within.
    Beyond these three statuses *Bhuvaneśvarī* has two more viz.

4. *Tirodāna*
5. *Anugraha*

The fourth task *Tirodāna* – the status of making the living things forgetting their individual *Ātma tattva*. Making the living things forget their *Āthma tattva* is called "*avidyā māyā*" (illusion of ignorance) by *Vedānta* texts. But this is also important. Based on the individual *karma*-s, *Śrī Devī* bestows joys and sorrows to all living beings. However, to enable the living beings to enjoy/ suffer the joys and sorrows the *Āthma tattva* has to be hidden. The presence of *Āthma tattva* in this world obstructs the enjoyment/ suffering of joys and sorrows. Hence it has to be hidden. In this state of ignorance, the living beings, could not do anything and destined to enjoy/ suffer based on their *prārabta karma*. Hence the task of *Tirodāna* is also a significant one.

Thus, the living beings drown and grasp in the ocean of this world. The compassionate *Śrī Devī* offers the living beings, *satsang* (interacting with virtuous society) and appropriate teacher. Thus, having obtained ardent, the human being reaches the teacher and receives the *mantra*-s of *Śrī Devī*, provoked by *Vedānta* thoughts, reaches a higher status. We have been seeing this in practice. Thus, *Śrī Devī* re-establishes the *Āthma tattva* to all proportionate to (based on) their level of devotion, *sādhana* and efforts. This is called *Anugraha*.

In this manner *Śrī Bhuvaneśvarī Devī* continuously performs all the 5 tasks. Hence, she is aptly called "*Pancakrutyaparāyaṇā* – पञ्चकृत्यपरायणा" (274th name in *Śrī Lalitā Sahasranāma*). Thus, indicates the *bījā Hrīm*.

The compassion of *Bhuvaneśvarī* falls on all without any blockage or barrier. **She** provides air to breath, water to drink, food to eat, proportionate heat to enjoy, earth to stay, *tattva*-s and appropriate teaches to develop in the life to all the living beings of these 14 worlds. Thus, **she** provides an environment to do *Upasana* for the human beings and continuous all **her** 5 tasks. This is cited by the *bījā Hrīm*. The '*īm*' here is a *kāmakalā bījā*. *Bhuvaneśvarī* satiates all the desires of those who chant it and also makes the status of no further desires.

It is mentioned in *Ṛg Veda* that only through the good *karmas* of past lives and grace of the *Guru* one can obtain *Bhuvaneśvarī Sādhana*. When Lord *Rāma* was being crowned his Guru *Vasishta* told him "Oh *Rām*! In this world of *Sādhana* there is no more powerful *Sādhana* for becoming prosperous than that of Goddess *Bhuvaneśvarī*.

Lord *Rāma* did just that and his reign was called *Rāmarājya*, in which there was prosperity and joy everywhere. Even Lord *Krishna* accomplished this *Sādhana* and was able to find the wonderful city of *Dwāraka* which was full of riches and wealth. Lord *Śiva* says that even a person who has been fated to be poor can become rich through this wonderful *Sādhana*. *Bhuvaneśvarī* is the Goddess who rules over the riches of the entire 14 worlds and **She** is worshipped even by the Gods and Yogis. The *Sādhak* gains respect and fame in the society and is honoured for his work. *Bhuvaneśvarī Sādhana* is a key to success in life no matter which field one has chosen.

This type of great form is *Bhuvaneśvarī*. Let us all worship **her** and get benefitted.

Tripurasundarī

Tripurasundarī (Beautiful Goddess of the Three worlds) or *Mahā-Tripurasundarī* (Great Beautiful [Goddess] of the Three worlds), also called *Ṣhoḍaśī* (Sixteen) or *Lalitā* (**She** Who Plays) or *Rājarājeśvarī* (Queen of Queens, Supreme Ruler), is one of the Daśa *Mahā Vidyā*-s (ten great forms of *Śrīdevī*). **She** is the foremost and the most important in among the ten. All other *vidyās* concludes in her *Vidyā* i.e. *Śrī Vidyā*. Her consort is *Mahā Kaneswaran*. *Lalitā Mahā Tripurasundarī* is the primary goddess associated with the *Shakta Tantric* tradition known as *Śrī Vidyā*.

It was earlier mentioned that the worship of *Śrī Vidyā*, begins with *Bālā*. After performing this *upāsanā* for a few years the *sādhaka* (devotee) can get the *Pancadaśī*, which is called as *mantra rājam* (king of *mantras*). Worshipping this *Pancadaśī* is very difficult. This is possible only with the kind compassion of a *Guru* (teacher). It was also earlier mentioned that this *mantra* has three groups viz., *vāgbhava*, *kāmarāja* and *śakti* groups. *Pancadaśī* has been mentioned in twelve different ways in multiple *tantras*. This has been obtained by various great sages after performing serious penances. Out of these the *khādi vidyā* started by Cupid (*Manmatha*) and *hādhi vidyā* started by *Lopāmudrā* wife of sage Agastya are most popular. *Śrī Bhāskararāya*, in his books called "*Soubhāgya Bhāskaram*" and "*Varivasya Rahasyam*" has categorically mentioned that *Khādi vidyā* is greater than *Hādhi vidyā*.

This *Pancadaśī mantra* is most powerful. By worshipping this *mantra*, one can get all the worldly desires and also liberation after death. This has been mentioned in *Śrī Durgā Saptaśatī* (13-4) also as "आराधिता सैव नृणां भोगस्वर्गापवर्गदा". Every letter in the *Pancadaśī mantra* is worthy of worshipping individually – says the book "*Vidyā Śoḍaśikārṇavam*" also called as "*Pūrva Catuśśatī*", by quoting different *tantra*-s. There is not even an iota of doubt that this *Pancadaśī* is capable providing *Aṇimādi siddhis* – all the *siddhis* starting from *Aṇimā*, to the devotees. However, people, who have mastered the *siddhis*, return to normal worldly life and become greedy of economic welfare, power, fame, pride, etc. In this process they completely ignore the ultimate goal of the worship viz., *Vedānta* knowledge and liberation.

Hence, this *Pancadaśī* is worshipped by prefixing the *Bālā bījās* to the three groups in this *mantra*. Such a *mantra* is called "*Soubhāgya Vidyā*". Akin to its name, this *mantra* bestows all the auspicious things to the worshippers. Its meditation verse (*dyāna ślokā*) describes the form of *Śrī Devī* to;

- Have four hands
- Be adored with the crescent Moon on **her** head.
- Have great, grand, breasts.
- Red in colour
- Have sugarcane bow and arrows made of flowers.

If a devotee, chant this *mantra* and worships *Śrī Devī* in *Śrī Cakra*, he will sequentially enjoy all the desires till liberation. When the *bījākṣar 'Śrīm'* is suffixed to this *mantra* it become *Ṣoḍaśī mantra* - *Pancadaśī* means fifteen and *Ṣoḍaśī* means sixteen. This has been confirmed by *Śrī Ullūka Bhaṭṭa* in his commentary for *Soundaryalaharī*. These two mantras are like two gems. The *Ṣoḍaśī mantra* destroys all the obstrucles in the path to liberation and takes the devotee to the highest level.

There is one other *mantra* in *Śrī Vidyā*, which is more powerful than this *Ṣoḍaśī mantra*. *Ṣoḍaśī* also refers to the sixteen-syllable *mantra*, which consists of the fifteen syllable (*pancadasākṣarī*) *mantra* plus a final seed syllable. Though there are 28 *bījā*-s (letters) in this *mantra*, it is considered to be having only 16 letters – says *tantras*. The reason being the three groups in the midst of the *śuddha Pancadaśī* mantra are accounted as three letters only. The first eight letters + the three letters in the form of three groups + the last five letters = sixteen letters that is *Ṣoḍaśī*. As *Ṣoḍaśī*, *Śrī Devī* is represented as a sixteen-year-old girl and is believed to embody sixteen types of desires. The *Ṣoḍaśī tantra* refers to *Ṣoḍaśī* as the "Beauty of the Three Worlds," or *Tripurasundarī*. There is a very popular saying among *Śrī Vidyā* tradition, which is that one has to be verily *Śiva* himself or in one's last birth to get initiated in *Śrī Vidyā*. Since everyone cannot be *Śiva*, it has to be the last birth, when one gets it, it becomes the last birth and one can worship *Lalitā* only if **she** wishes him to do so.

The *Ṣoḍaśī mantra* is also called as *Mahāṣoḍaśī* in *tantras*. This *Devī* of *Mahāṣoḍaśī* is termed as *Lalitā*, one among the *Daśa Mahā Vidyā*. All *mantra*-s are considered secretive in nature and more so for *śākta mantra*-s. *Ṣoḍaśī* is no way an exception. Recitation of *Ṣoḍaśī* leads to liberation. This does not give any materialistic gains. It leads straight to the *Brahmam* – *Brahmagnānam* = knowledge of *Brahmam*.

The dwelling places of *Śrī Devī* are:

- The heart of an ardent devotee
- The *Bindu*, the center of the *Śrī Cakra*.

Though she is omnipresent in the form *parā*, **she** resides in the *Bindu* by accommodating the request of the devotee. **She** dwells on the body of the *Sadāśivā*, on the cot called *"Panca Manjika"*, in the *Bindu*, the center of the *Śrī Cakra*. The four legs of this cot are *Brahmā*, *Viṣṇu*, *Rudra* and *Īsāna* and the sitting plank or bed spread is *Sadāśivā*. These four legs added to the bed spread

indicate the five tasks performed by *Śrī Devī*. Thus, having delegated the five tasks to five individuals, **she** happily rests. Hence, **she** is called in *Śrī Lalitā Sahasranāma* as *Pancapretāsanāsīnā* – पञ्चप्रेतासनासीना (58th name) and again as *Pancabrahmāsanastitā* – पञ्चब्रह्मासनस्तिता (249th name). The five functions, as already discussed, are:

1. Creation (*Sruṣṭi*)
2. Sustenance (*Stiti*)
3. Destruction (*Samhāra*) – including all the worlds within self
4. Screaming from the impacts of material pleasure & displeasure (*Tirodhāna*) – making the living beings forget about their own self, on account ignorance and worldly pleasures
5. Blessings (*Anugraha*) to bring about the changes – to liberate the living beings by knowledge obtained through appropriate *guru*-s, by teaching the *Veda* sentences.

Hence, it is evident that every activity in all beings is on account of *Śrī Devī* only. That is the reason, **she** is called as *śakti* (energy). No being can do anything with energy.

The inner tattva meaning of the weapons in her hand are:

1. *Pāśa* (noose) – the desires of the human beings
2. *Ankuśa* (goad) – the anger, which is uncontrollable by a human being
3. The uncontrollable mind of the devotees is indicated as a sugar cane bow.
4. The five elements utilized by all beings in this world are indicated as five arrows made of flowers.

The charm of the form of *Śrī Devī* has been beautifully described by Vāg *Devīs* in *Śrī Lalitā Sahasra-nāma*. It is normal convention to describe the form of Gods from toe to head. On the contrary it has been described from head to toe in in *Śrī Lalitā Sahasranāma*. The reason being - *Śrī Devī* originated from *Cidagni Kuṇḍa*. When **she** comes out of the holy fire, the head comes out first and the entire form is seen from head to toe and hence the description is also.

The maximum benefit reaped by a worshipper of *Mahāṣoḍaśī* is the knowledge about *Śiva – Śivagnānam*. Hence, **she** is aptly called as *Śivagnānapradāyinī* – शिवज्ञानप्रदायिनी in *Śrī Lalitā Sahasranāma* (727th name).

It is more perfect to worship the form of this *Mahāṣoḍaśī*, locating her in Bindu, the center point of *Śrī Cakra*, as a part of special *argyā* (*tarpaṇa*). This has mentioned in *Śrī Lalitā Sahasranāma* as *Bindutarpaṇasantuṣṭā* - बिन्दुतर्पणसंतुष्टा (974th name). There are various prescriptions in this *upāsanā* – the important one being – ladies should not be dishonored at any point of time. All ladies are in the form of *Śrī Devī*. *Śrī Durgā*

Saptaśatī" (11-6) also says "विद्या: समस्तास्तव देवि भेदा: स्त्रिय: समस्ता सकला जगत्सु ।".

Sumangali-s (ladies living with husband) worshipping *Śrī Devī* and worshipping *sumangali* ladies in the form of *Śrī Devī* are all part and parcel of *Srividya*. Many a *Śākta* text has affirmed this as a great form of worship. *Śrī Lalitā Sahasranāma* in this regard, says (967th name) *Sumangalī* - सुमङ्गली and again as (971st name), *Suvāsinyarcanaprītā* – सुवासिन्यर्चनप्रीता. This is one of the easiest ways for a human being to raise his level of life. Thus, great mantra is *Mahāṣoḍaśī.*

A *mantra* above this *Mahāṣoḍaśī* is called *Parāṣoḍaśī mantra*. In general, this is called as *Parā*. This *mantra* is most helpful to get rid of from the birth and death cycle and to reach emancipation. Only after chanting the *Mahāṣoḍaśī mantra* for 45 lakhs times, one devotee becomes eligible to get this mantra initiated. This *mantra* has only one *bīja* or letter. Still worshipping this *mantra* is very difficult. There are very few devotees who worship *Mahāṣoḍaśī* and all the rarer is for whom *guru*-s have taught *Parā mantra.*

The meditation verse (*dhyāna śloka*) for *Parāṣoḍaśī Devi* reads as:

चापं चेक्षुमयं प्रसूनविशिकां पाशांकुशौ
पुस्तकम् माणिक्याक्ष सरोरुहं मणिमयीं
वीणां सरोजत्वयम् ।
हस्ताब्जैस्तु वराभयेश ददतीं ब्रह्मादि
सेव्यां पराम् सिन्दूरारुण विग्रहां बगवतीं तां
षोढशीं बावये ॥

This describes that *Parāṣoḍaśī Devi* has to be meditated as to be Red in colour and having 12 hands – 1. A noose, 2. A hoad, 3. A book, 4. *akṣa mālā* (a garland of gem stones), 5-6. Veena (a string instrument), 7-8. Lotus flower, 9. *Abhaya* (removal of fears) *mudra*, 10. *Vara mudra* (offering boons), 11. Sugarcane and 12. Five arrows made of flowers.

Normally mantra-s are initiated through three methods viz., *Śākti dīkṣā*, *Śāmbavī dīkṣā* and *mantra dīkṣā*. But, the *parā mantra* can be obtained only by *Veda* and *antarmukha dīkṣā*-s through an appropriate *guru*. The teacher should ensure that the disciple has deep dedication to *Guru* and clarity & cleanliness in the mind, before initiating *parā mantra* to the disciple. Thus, glory of *Śrīdevī* has been enjoyed by *devatas* and sages in groups. Only with the great compassion of *Śrīdevī*, one can become *Śrīvidyā Upāsaka*. The magnificence of *Śrīdevī* cannot be completely articulated by anyone. It has to be reached through an appropriate and learned *Guru*. The guru, who initiates the *Śrīvidyā Upāsana* to anyone, should have learnt *Vedas* in a proper way, learnt the rules of *Sāstra*-s and strictly follow the self-discipline and rules of *Sāstra*. He should also be strict follower of religion and self-rules. He should be a great person leading a contended life, should have compassion on his disciples. Such a great guru having devotion on *Śrīdevī* and with her permission can initiate the *Śrīvidyā* to the students. There is one more important prescription be the *Śrīvidyā* is taught. The student should ask for it from the teacher and the teacher should not initiate himself. This has been confirmed in *Brahmāṇḍa Purāṇā* as *Bhagavān Hayagrīva* as *guru* and sage Agastya as disciple.

Let us firmly get hold of the holy feet of such *guru*-s and the lotus feet of *Śrīdevī* and by doing crores of humble *pranāms* to them and their blessings and wishes.

Let *Śrīdevī* shower her limitless compassion on everyone for a long, happy and peaceful contented life in this world and liberation afterwards.

*****

Chaṇḍī – Three Great *Devis*

Sri Devi Mahatmyam can mean singing of the greatness of *Sri Devi*. This text has 700 verses and hence it is called as *Saptashatee* (*Sapta* = 7 + *Shatee* = 100) – also called as *Durga Saptashatee*. Each of these verses is a *mantra* – hence *Chandi yagna* is being performed with these *mantras*. Hence this text itself is called as *Chandee*. This is read amidst *Markandeya Purana*. Hence, in some schools, it is mentioned that this has been written by sage *Markandeya*. However, all the *purana*-s are written sage Veda Vyasa and hence naturally this text also.

Sri Devi Maahaatmyam is in the form sage *Sumetas*[15] narrating the story of Sri Devi (destroying the demons) to a king called Suradan and to a *Vaishya* (businessman) called *Samaathi*. Upon hearing the story, Samaathi got matured and continued his remaining life worshipping Sri Devi. On the other hand, Suradan got back his kingdom and later he is going to be one of the future *Manu*-s and will become the head of a *manvantara*.

The story has been divided into three – *Pratama* (first), *Madhyama* (middle) and *Uttama* (last) *charitrams*. These *charitrams* respectively belong to *Mahakalee*, *Mahalakshmi* and *Mahasaraswati*. It is being attempted to know something about these 3 *Devis*. Devis relating the remaining 10 chapters will be discussed in the next chapter.

Devi puja is performed stating that *Chandi* is the combined form of *Mahakalee*, *Mahalakshmi* and *Mahasaraswati*. This means that each of those *Devis*. Let us all realize this and understand about each of the them.

Usually, the *Dhyana* verse of the Deities will explain the form of the concerned God.

An analytical table about *Sri Devi Maahaatmyam*;

---

[15] Some people say that this is sage *Vashishtar*

	Pratama charitram	Madhyama Charitram	Uttama Charitram
Chapters	1	2, 3 & 4	From 5 to 13
Sage	Brahma	Vishnu	Rudran
Form of Ambika	Mahakalee	Mahalakshmi	Mahasaraswati
Form of Sri Devi	Sat	Chit	Aanandam
Veda@@	Rig	Yajur	Saama
Role of Ambika	Behind the scene	Alone	Alongwith with other *Devis* created by **her**
Demons Destroyed	Madhu & Kaidabha	Mahishaasuran	Dhoomralocanan, Chandan, Mundan, Raktabeejan, Nishumban & Shumban

@@ As a prelude to *Sri Devi Maahaatmyam*, *Devi Kavaca*, *Arkalaa* and *Keelaka* stotras are chant and for concluding *Rahasyatraya mantras* are chant. These are all from *Atharva* Veda.

This implies that, chanting of *Sri Devi Maahaatmyam* will mean that all the 4 Vedas are chant.

1. *Sri Mahakalee*

The presiding deity of the first charitram is *Sri Mahakalee*. Her *Dhyana* verse is;

ॐ खड्गं चक्रगदेषुचापपरिघाञ्छूलं भुशुण्डीं शिरः
शङ्खं सन्दधतीं करैस्त्रिनयनां सर्वाङ्गभूषावृताम् ।
नीलाश्मद्युतिमास्यपाददशकां सेवे महाकालिकां
यामस्तौत्स्वपिते हरौ कमलजो हन्तुं मधुं कैटभम् ॥

Om Khadgam Cakra Gadeşucāpa Parighānchūlam Bhuśuņḍīm Śiraḥ
Śankham Sandadhatīm Karaistrinayanām Sarvānga Bhūşāvrutām |
Nīlāśmadyutimāsya Pādadaśakām Seve Mahākālikām
Yāmastoutsvapite Harou Kamalajou Hantum Madhum Kaiţabham ||

I serve that *Mahā Kālikā*, who is three eyed, wearing ornaments in all parts of body, in the colour of deep blue sapphire having ten faces and ten legs. She holds Sword, Discus, mace, Bow and arrow, Iron club, Trident, Catapult, Severed head and Conch, in her ten hands. (Sword, discus, arrow, severed head and conch are on her right hands - Mace, bow, Iron club, trident and catapult in her left hands).

She has thirty eyes in her ten heads. She woke up Lord Vishnu by the prayers of *Brahma* for annihilation of demons *Madhu* and *Kaitabha*.

She is in the form of '*Sat*', the end of the end.

This goddess removes all the obstacles that appear in the contempt and outcasts of her devotees. To completely destroy the character of *Tamas*, she displays the characteristic blackness. In the *Pratama Charitram* in *Sri Devi Mahatmya*, behind the scene, she helped *Sri Maha-Vishnu* to destroy the twin-demons *Madhu-Kaidaban*, who originated from his ear-wax.

2. *Sri Mahalakshmi*

The presiding deity of the middle charitram is *Sri Mahalakshmi*. Her *Dhyana* verse is;

ॐ अक्षस्रक्परशू गदेषुकुलिशं पद्मं धनुः कुण्डिकां
दण्डं शक्तिमसिं च चर्म जलजं घण्टां सुराभाजनम् ।
शूलं पाशसुदर्शने च दधतीं हस्तैः प्रवालप्रभां
सेवे सैरिभमर्दिनीमिह महालक्ष्मीं सरोजस्थिताम् ॥

Om. Akśasrak Paraśum Gadesu Kuliśam Padmam Dhanuḥ Kuṇḍikām
Daṇḍam Śaktimasim Ca Carma Jalajam Ghantām Surābhājanam |
Śūlam Pāśa Sudarśane Ca Dadhattīm Hastaiḥ Prasannānanam
Seve Sairibha Mardinī Miha Mahālakśmīm Sarojasthitām ||

First of all, all of us must keep in mind that this *Lakshmi* is different from another of *Sri Vishnu*'s companion – she originated from ocean of milk. She is the one who bestows all wealth. This *Mahalakshmi* is different – one of features of *Chandi*.

Born out of the combined powers of all devas, being in the colour of coral (red hue), she holds – Rosary, lotus, arrow, sword, thunderbolt, mace, discus, ceremonial water pot, conch in her right hands;

Axe, Mace, bow, rod, spear, bell, cup with liquor, trident and rope in her left hands.

- Rosary – Japamāla – made of spatika – given by Brahma
- Axe – given by Vishwakarma
- Mace – given by Vishnu
- Arrow – given by Vayu deva]
- Thunderbolt – given by Indra
- Lotus – given by Samudra raja
- Bow – given by Vayu deva
- Ceremonial water pot (Kamaṇḍalu) – given by Brahma
- Rod – given by Yama-dharma raja
- Spear – given by Agni
- Sword – given by Kala deva
- Shield - given by Kala deva
- Conch – given by Varuṇa deva
- Bell – given by Airāvata – Indra's mount elephant

- Cup filled with liquor – given by Kubera
- Trident – given by Śiva
- Rope – given by Varuṇa deva
- Discus – given by Vishnu

She is seated on a lotus with a bright smiling face to bless her devotees. She is in the form of 'Chit'.

She alone, probably with the help of her vehicle, lion, killed the thousands of army men and the demon Mahishaasura. Thus, destroyed the distress of the *Devas*.

3. *Sri Mahasaraswati*

The presiding deity of the *Utama (Uttara)* charitram is *Sri Mahasaraswati*. Her *Dhyana* verse is;

ॐ घण्टाशूलहलानि शङ्खमुसले चक्रं धनुः सायकं

हस्ताब्जैर्दधतीं घनान्तविलसच्छीतांशुतुल्यप्रभाम् ।

गौरीदेहसमुद्भवां त्रिजगतामाधारभूतां

महा-पूर्वामत्र सरस्वतीमनुभजे शुम्भादिदैत्यार्दिनीम् ॥

Gantā Śūla Halāni Śankhamusale Cakram Dhanuḥ Sāyakam
Hastābjairdadhatīm Ghanāntavilasacchītām Śutulya Prabhām |
Gowrī Deha Samudbhavām Trijagatām Ādhārabhūtām
Mahā Pūrvāmatra Sarasvatīmanubhaje Śumbhādidaityaardinīm ||

This Devi is also called as *Koushikee*. She is not that *Saraswathi* who is a consort of Lord Brahma. She is in-charge of learning. This *Devi* also is capable of bestowing education. But she is a form of *Chandi*.

With the brightness and colour of the hue of a Rising Sun, wearing red garments and a garland of skulls. Her breast is anointed with blood and she holds in her eight hands, a rosary, a book and showing gestures of dispelling fear and granting boons. She is three eyed and has an auspicious lotus like face. The playful deity is having a crescent of moon in her crown.

She as the head of army of *Sri Devi* created the seven mothers and other *Devis*, killed the entire army and the demons like *Dhoomralochanan, Chandan, Mundan, Raktabeejan, Nishumban* and *Shumban*.

Thus, **she** in the form of '*Anandam*', the endless bliss, destroyed the sorrows of the *Devas*.

Thus, *Sri Chandi*, great *Devi*, incarnated as three different deities, to help the devas. At the beginning of the *Sri Lalita Sahasranama*, we read the 5th name as, the *Devakaarya Samutyuta*. However, as the "*Sat Chit Ananda*" form, the devotees not only satiated with their needs, but are also blessed by her great mercy.

*****

Saptaśatī* Chapter *Devis

There are presiding deities (*Devis*) for each of the 13 chapters of *Sri Durga Saptashatee*;

1. *Sri Mahaa Kaali – Mahaa Maayaa*
2. *Sri Mahaa Lakshmi - Sarvasyaadyaa*
3. *Sri Tripura Bhairavee – Mahaa Vidyaa*
4. *Sri Jaya Durgaa*
5. *Sri Mahaa Saraswathi*
6. *Sri Padmaavati – Nandaa*
7. *Sri Matangi - Shaakambari*
8. *Sri Bhavani – Rakta Dhantikaa*
9. *Sri Arddhaambikaa - Bheema*
10. *Sri Kaameshwari - Braamari*
11. *Sri Bhuvaneshwari*
12. *Sri Agni Durgaa*
13. *Sri Shivaa*

Out of the above, the 1st, 2nd and 5th *Devis* viz. *Sri Mahakalee, Sri Mahalakshmi* and *Sri Mahasaraswati* have been understood in the previous chapter. Let us try to visualize other *Devis*.

As a suffix to *Sri Devi Maahaatmyam* it is usual to chant *Rahasyatrayam* (three secret verses). These verses describe the forms/ images of the above *Devis*. Each *Devi* is a *tatvam*. The inner subtle nuances of those *tattvas* have also been described in the *Rahasyatrayam*.

<u>Devi of 3rd Chapter - *Sri Tripura Bhairavee*</u>

ओं उद्यद्भानु सहस्र कान्ति-मरुण-क्षौमां शिरो मालिकाम्
रक्तालिप्त-पयोधरां जपवटीं विद्यामभीतिं वरम् ।
हस्ताब्जैर्-दधतीं त्रिनेत्र विलसद् वक्त्रारविन्दश्रियम्
देवीं बद्ध हिमाम्शु रत्नमुकुटां वन्देऽरविन्दस्तिताम् ॥

Om Udyadbhānu Sahasra Kānti-maruṇakśoumām Śiro Mālikām
Raktālipt-Payodharām Japavatīm Vidyāmabhītim Varam I
Hastābjair-dadhatīm Trinetra Vilasad Vaktrāravindaśriyam

Devīm Baddh Himāṃśu Ratnamukutām Vanderavindastitām ‖

Of the hue of Rising Sun, wearing red garments, wearing a garland of skulls her breast is anointed with blood holding in her hands a rosary, book and showing gestures of dispelling fear and granting boons, three eyed in her auspicious lotus like face, the playful deity having a crescent of moon in her crown seated on a lotus, I bow in reverence.

This is the *Devi*, who killed the demon *Mahishaasuran*.

Devi of 4th Chapter - *Sri Jaya Durgaa*

ॐ - कालाभ्राभां कटाक्षैररि कुलभयदां मौलिबद्धेन्दुरेखां
शंखं चक्रं कृपाणं त्रिशिखमपि करैरुद् वहन्तीं त्रिनेत्राम् ।
सिंहस्कन्धाधिरूढां त्रिभुवनमखिलं तेजसा पूरयन्तीं ध्यायेद् दुर्गां
जयाख्यां त्रिदशपरिवृतां सेवितां सिद्धिकामै: ‖

Om - Kālābhrāpām Kaṭākśairari Kulabhayadām Moulipaddhēndu Rēkhām Śaṅkham Cakram Krupāṇam Triśikamapi Karairud Vahantīm Trinētrām |
Simhaskandhādhirūḍhām Tribhuvanamakhilam Tējasā

Pūrayantīm Dyāyēd Durgām Jayākyām
Tridaśaparivrutām Sēvitām Siddhiikāmaiḥ ॥

Devas praise the *Sri Devi*, who destroyed the demon, *Mahishaasura* with his entire army. Goddess accepts the same.

Of the rain bearing cloud's hue (dark), causing fear with her glances to her hoard of enemies, fixed a crescent in her crown, holding in her hands a conch, discus, sword and trident with great fervour, three eyed, riding on a lion, filling all the three worlds with her radiance, I meditate on Durga called as *'Jaya'*, attended by the devas (who are thirty three crores in number), worshipped by devotees who want the siddhis.

<u>*Devi* of 6th Chapter - *Sri Padmaavati*</u>

ॐ नागाधीश्वर विष्टरां फणि फणोत्त सोरुरत्नावली
भास्वद्देहलतां दिवाकरनिभां नेत्रत्रयोद्भासिताम् ।
माला कुंभ कपाल नीरजकरां चन्द्रार्धचूडांबरां सर्वज्ञेश्वर
भैरवांकनिलयां पद्मावर्तीं चिन्तये ॥

Om Nāgādhīśvar Viṣṭarām Phani Phaṇotta Soruratnāvalee
Bhāsvaddehalatān Divākaranibhān Netratrayodbhāsitām ।
Māla Kumbh Kapāl Neerajakarān Chandrārdhachoodāmbarān
Sarvagyeshvar Bhairavānkanilayān Padmāvateen Chintaye ॥

This is the *Devi*, who flew the monster named *Dhoomralochanan* as a smoke.

Having the lord of Snakes as her seat, wearing a snake hood like jeweled ornaments on her feet, thus shining brightly, of Sun's hue, having splendorous three eyes, having a rosary, pot, skull and lotus in her hands, having a crescent in her head (crown), the highest consciousness, seated on the lap of *Sarvagnesvara Bhairava*, I think in my mind - meditate that *Devi* called *Padmavati*.

Devi of 7th Chapter - *Sri Mātangi*

ॐ ध्यायेयं रत्नपीठे शुककलपठितं शृण्वतीं श्यामलाङ्गीं
न्यस्तैकाङ्घ्रिं सरोजे शशिशकलधरां वल्लकीं वादयन्तीं ।
कह्लारा बद्धमालां यमितविलसच्चोलिकां रक्तवस्त्रां
मातङ्गीं शङ्खपात्राम् मधुरमधुमदां चित्रकोद्भासि भालाम् ॥

Om Dhyāyeyan Ratnapīṭhai Śukakalapaṭhitam Śrunvatīn Śyāmalāngīm

Nyastaikānghrim Saroje Śaśiśakaladharām Vallakīm Vādayantīm |
Kahlārā Baddhamālām Yamitavilasachcholikām Raktavastrām
Mātangīm Śankhapātrām Madhuramadhumadām Chitrakodbhāsi Bhālām ||

This Devi slaughtered the twin demons *Chandan* and *Mundan*. Thus, she completed the task for the *Devas*.

I meditate upon that *Devi*, who is seated on gem studded seat, hearing the parrot's voice of dark hue, keeping her foot on a lotus, wearing a crescent, playing the stringed veena, wearing a garland of lotus/ white lily, her hair is braided, wearing red garments, *Matangi Devi*, also holding a conch, smiling sweetly, varied bright coloured shades are emitting from her fore head.

<u>*Devi* of 8th Chapter - *Sri Bhavāni*</u>

ॐ अरुणां करुणा तरङ्गिताक्षीं धृत पाशाङ्कुश पुष्प बाणचापाम् ।
अणिमादिभि रावृतां मयूखैरह मित्येव विभावये भवानीम् ॥

Om Aruṇām Karuṇā Tarangitakśīm Dhruta Pāśankuśa Puşpa
Bānacāpām ।
Animādibhi Rāvrutām Mayukhairah Mityeva Vibhāvaye
Bhawānīm ॥

In the form of *Kali*, *Devi* drank each drop of blood oozing out of the demon *Raktabeejan*, and then destroyed him to bless the *Devas*.

Of the rising sun's hue, with compassion filled glances like waves from her eyes, holding the noose, goad, (flowery) arrows and (sugarcane) bow in her hands, surrounded by *Devi's* starting from *anima* (*avarana devata*), who are personification of the rays emitting from her.

Devi of 9th Chapter - *Sri Arddhaambikaa*

ॐ - बन्धूक काञ्चन निभं रुचिराक्षमालां पाशाङ्कुशौ च वरदां निजबाहुदण्डै: ।

बिभ्राणमिन्दु शकला भरणं त्रिनेत्र मर्धाबिकेश मनिशं वपुराश्रयामि ॥

Om - Bandhūka Kānchana Nibham Ruchirākśamālām
Pāśānkuśou Cha Varadām Nijabāhudandaiḥ ।
Bibhrāṇamindu Śakalā Bharaṇam Trinetra
Mardhāmbikeśa Maniśam Vapurāśrayāmi ॥

One half of the body is red like the banduka flower and other is golden, holding in the hands a rosary, noose, goad and gesture of dispelling fear, wearing a crescent as an ornament, three eyes, half female and half male body, always, I seek refuge.

Devi of 10th Chapter - *Sri Kaameshwari*

ॐ -उत्तप्त हेम रुचिरां रवि चन्द्र वह्नि

नेत्रां दनुश् शरयुतां कुश पाश शूलम् ।

रम्यैर्भुजैश्च दधतीं शिव शक्ति रूपां

कामेश्वरीं हुदि भजामि धृतेन्दु लेखाम् ॥

Om - Uttapta Hema Ruchirām Ravi Chandra Vahni
Netrām Danuś Śarayutām Kuśa Pāśa Śūlam ।
Ramyairbhujaiścha Dadhatīm Śiva Śakti Rūpām
Kāmeśvarīm Hrudi Bhajāmi Dhrutendu Lekhām ॥

The Goddess who blessed the Devas by destroying the monster, *Shumban*.

Of the hue of molten gold, having the sun moon and fire as her three eyes, in her elegant hands holding a bow, arrow, goad and trident. Of the unified powers of *Shiva* and *Shakti*, I worship *Kameshvari* in my heart, who wears a piece of moon- crescent (in her crown).

Devi of 11th Chapter - *Sri Bhuvaneshwari*

ॐ - बालरवि द्युति मिन्दुकिरीटां तुङ्गकुशां नयनत्रय युक्ताम् ।
स्मेरमुखीम् वरदाङ्कुश पाशा भीतिकरां प्रभजे भुवनेशीम् ॥

Om - Bālaravi Dyuti Mindukirīṭām Tungakuśām Nayanatraya

Yuktām I

Smeramukhīm Varadānkuśa Pāśā Bhītikarām Prabhaje

Bhuvaneśīm II

The goddess accepts the gratitude of all the *Devas* who praised her for annihilating the nymphs *Nishumban*, *Shumban* and all.

Of the young rising sun's hue having a crescent on her crown, with big breasts, having three eyes, with a smiling face, in her hands are the noose, goad and gestures of removing fear and bestowing grace. I worship with fervour *Devi Bhuvaneshvari*.

Devi of 12th Chapter - *Sri Agni Durgaa*

ॐ - विद्युद्धाम समप्रभां मृगपतिस्कन्धस्थितां भीषणां
कन्याभि: करावाल खेट विलसद्धस्ताभि रासेविताम् ।
हस्तैश् चक्र गदासि खेट विशिखांश्चापं गुणं तर्जनीं
बिभ्राणा मनलात्मिकां शशिधरां दुर्गां त्रिनेत्रां भजे ॥

Om – Vidyuddhāma Samaprabhām Mrugapati Skandhasthitām
                                                    Bhīṣanām

Kanyābhiḥ Karāvāla Kheṭa Vilasaddhastābhi Rāsevitām |
Hastaiś Chakra Gadāsi Kheṭa Viśikhāmśchāpam Gunam Tarjanīm
Bibhrāṇa Manalātmikām Śaśidharām Durgām Trinetrām Bhaje ||

Shining like a lighting, riding the king of animals – Lion served by maidens who carry a sword and shield and look fierce, having in her hands discus, mace, sword, shield, arrows, bow, trident and the gesture showing the index finger – that of making a threat.
Like a fire wearing the crescent, I worship that Three eyed Devi Durga.

Generally, for any *stotra*-s, the fruits part (*phala shruti*) will be an appendix, normally written by someone else or sometime later. But in the case of *Sri Devi Maahaatmyam*, *phala shruti* is part of the text and in particular it is in the form of the voice of *Sri Devi* **Herself.**

She lists down the benefits of chanting *Sri Devi Maahaatmyam*. She also says that the same benefits can be obtained just by hearing someone chanting the stotra. One step further, even if the stotra is just reminded off, that person will get the same fruits.

Sri Krishna, in his *Bhagavad Gita*, assured *"Sambavaami Yuge Yuge"* – will take incarnations as and when the devotees are in trouble. Similarly, Sri Devi also assures Devas that she will arise whenever they are in distress. She also informs in advance that she will incarnate in the house of Nandagopa as daughter of Yashoda during *Dvapara yug*.

Devi of 13th Chapter - *Sri Shivaa*

ॐ - बालार्क मण्डला भासां चतुर्बाहुं त्रिलोचनाम् ।
पाशांगुश वराभीतिर्धारयन्तीं शिवां भजे ॥

Om - Bālārka Maṇḍalā Bhāsām Chaturbāhum Trilochanām ।
Pāśānguśa Varābhītirdhārayantīm Śivām Bhaje ॥

Having a brightness of young sun, four armed, three eyed, holding in her hands are the noose, goad, and gestures of removing fear and bestowing grace, the auspicious one called *Shivaa*, I worship.

Sri Ambika, as a blessing to the devas, bestows a variety of boons to the devotees like us. Let us all soaked in the rain of such boons.

Devi Mahatmyam Durga Saptasati

*****

Daśa Mahā Vidyā Devis

There are 'n' number of images of *Devi*-s worshipped by sages for quite a long time. The most significant ten among them are being discussed in this chapter.

Each of these ten *vidya*-s is called *Brahma Vidya*. *Tantra sastras* describe in detail the worshipping methods of these *Devis*.

Out of these 10 *vidya*-s, the *Tripura Sundari Vidya* also called as *Sri Vidya* is more famous in South India.

The mantra, yantra, dyana, worshipping methods, results, forms, etc., of these ten vidya-s can be seen in the tantra texts. Sir Arthur Avalon, has also explained in detail in English.

There are different types in the worship of *Sri Devi* – like *Vaamaachaara*, *Dakshinaachaara*, *Samayaachaara* and *Koulachaara*. Sri Lalita Sahasranama[16] is accepted by all these methods.

The destruction of *Daksha*'s *yagna* by *Sati Devi* has been described in the 4th *Skanda* of *Shrimad Bhagavatam*. This has also been described in detail in *Bruhat Dharma Purana*. Once when *Daksha Prajapati* was proceeding towards the *yagna Shala* (the place where the holy fire was being conducted), Lord *Shiva* (his son-in-law), who was in meditation did not get up as a respect. On account of this *Daksha* got wild and gave a curse that Lord Shiva will not get any share from the *yagna*. From that moment onwards, Lord Shiva does not even see Daksha.

In another instance, Daksha Prajapati himself started a *yagna*. All his daughters were invited with their husbands excepting *Sati Devi*. Knowing this, **she** asked permission from her husband Lord Shiva to attend the *yagna*, executed by his father. When Lord Shiva did not permit her, **she** took the form of *Mahaa Kaalee*.

---

[16] *Sri Lalita Sahasranama* – 98th name – *Samayaachaaratatparaa*, 441st name – *Koulamaarga Tatpara Sevitaa*

Surprised by the most terrified form of peaceful *Sati Devi*, Lord *Shiva* started running from that place. But in whichever direction he ran, *Devi* was before him with the terrified form. The ten forms **She** took in all the ten directions (8 directions + upward + downward) are *Devi's Maha Vidyas*.

Surprised by this Lord Shiva stood stunned. Though *Devi* tried to console him stating that **She** is *Sati Devi* only, Lord *Shiva* could not get away from the fear immediately. Then *Devi* explained the specialties and purposes of all the ten *Vidya*-s to her husband.

Further **She** mentioned – "the *Vedas* and sacred writings (*Agamas*) told by you to this world are my two hands. I wear moveable and immoveable things of this world with those two hands. These ten forms will help to bless the worshippers. People should reach me by secretly following the *mantra*, *yantra*, verses, *kavacha*, etc., as taught by the teacher. I am telling you with the affection on you. Please permit me to attend the *yagna*" – **She** requested.

After getting his permission, **she** reached the *yagna* place of Daksha, which was protected by Nandi, Bringi and others. **She** could not tolerate the reprimands on Lord Shiva and hence disappeared in the fire of *yoga*. Knowing this Lord Shiva created *Virabhadra* from his entangled locks of hair and sent him to destroy the *yagna* of Daksha. *Devi* also took the form of *Badrakaalee* and with the help of *Veerabhadra* destroyed Daksha and all the opponents of Lord Shiva. This is the reason for the origination of Dasha *Maha Vidyas*[17].

Out of the three qualities of illusion, the pure *sattva* quality related with *Brahmam* (the Supreme Being) is called *Vidya*. Arthur Avalon feels that even in this the fourth and which is beyond any *tattva* is the blissful form of *Devi* is called *Maha Vidya*.

---

[17] This author has penned a separate book on *Dasha Mahā Vidyā* in English

Chamunda tattva splits these ten *Mahavidyas* into *Mahavidyas*, *Siddhavidyas* and *Vidyas*. But *Shyama Rahasya* mentions all these as *Mahavidyas* only. We also follow this and call all the ten as *Mahavidyas*.

The directions in which the ten *Mahavidyas* originated are described in the below diagram.

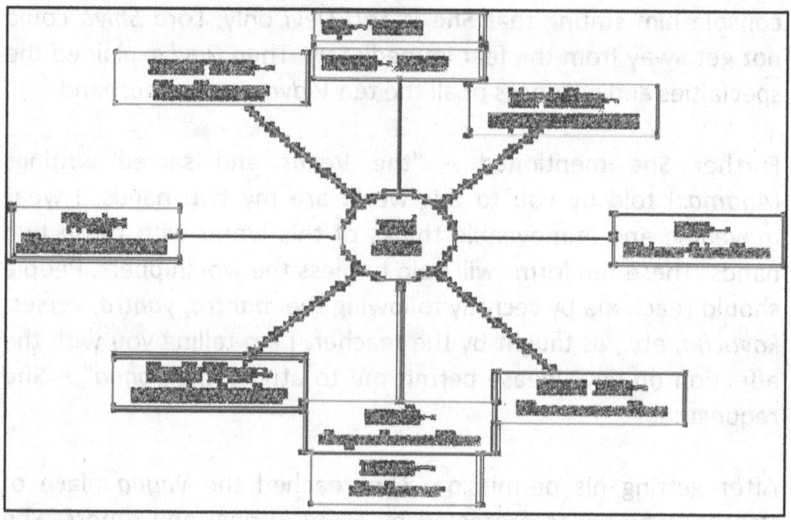

Let us try to understand a little about each of these 10 Devis. The image and chakra of the Devis are also indicated for easier comprehensiveness.

1.   *Śrī Mahā Kālī*

The form of *Kaalee* – **She** is black in colour and in ferocious form. **She** wears a garland of 51 skulls (indicating 51 root letters [*beeja aksharas*]). Her blooded long tongue is protruding outwards. **She** holds a trunk in one hand and a blood-stained sword in another. **She** keeps one leg on the corpse of *Shiva*.

During the *maha pralaya* time – the entire universe is dissolute and destructed. The whole world is like a cemetery. Kaalee is the only one who is and hence immortal.

Sri Devi Mahatmyam (*Saptashati*) says – *Kali* helped *Sri Devi* to kill the demon called *Raktabija*.

Devi originating herself in ten different forms protect whole of this world. Out of the ten *Mahavidyas*, the *Kali Vidya* is the first one. This *Devi* is being worshipped in India in the places like Bengal, Andhra and *Kama Roopa* regions. *Kalidas* and *Ramakrishna Paramahamsa* are instances of devotees who worshipped *Kali* and obtained boundless graces and became very great in their lives.

2. *Śrī Tārā* (Blue *Saraswathi*)

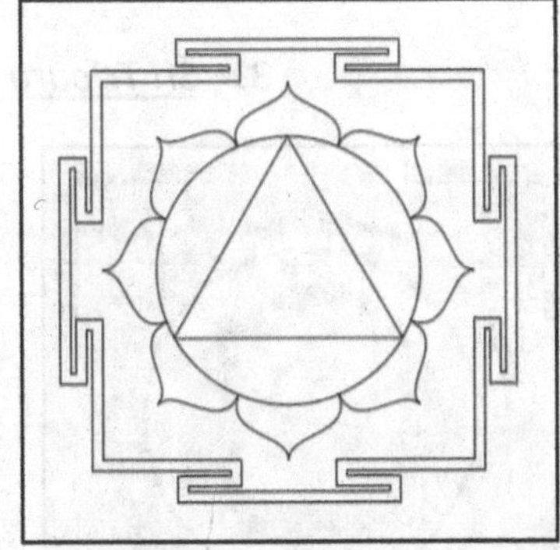

Shakta tantras talk about 11 nights; *Kalaratri, Veeraratri, Moharatri, Maharatri, Krodaratri, Goraratri, Taraaratri, Abalaratri, Tarunaratri, Sivaratri* and *Divyaratri*.

Out of these, *Tara* originated in *Kalaratri* – *Narakachaturdashi* (Diwali) day. The New Moon (*Amavasya*) relating to this *Kalaratri* is optimal to *Tara*.

If Tuesday, New Moon and *Kalaratri* fall on a same day, the devotees of *Tara* feel very happy. That is a very rare occasion.

*Shakta Tantra*s say that *Tara Devi* herself incarnated as *Rama* and Lord *Shiva* incarnated as *Sita*. 'Raa' means *Shakti* and 'Maa' means *Shiva*. Hence *Rama* is the *Parabrahma* form of *Shiva-Shakti*. There is story behind this.

Ravana was a very great devotee of Lord *Shiva*. Once he shaked and lifted the Mount *Kailash* itself. Scared of this, *Parvati* hugged *Shiva*. She was also angry that *Shiva* did not condemn *Ravana*. *Shiva* replied that he was enjoying the hug of his consort. *Parvati* said that she also wanted to enjoy that feeling. Lord *Shiva* said to *Parvati* "you incarnate as *Rama* and I will incarnate as *Sita*. After the killing of demons *Kara* and others, I will hug you and you will enjoy that feeling".

During the dissolution of the universe, Brahma was borne from the naval of Lord Vishnu. Brahma wanted to learn Vedas. Vishnu asked him to worship *Tara* (*Blue Sarasvati*), who will bestow all the 4 Vedas.

3.   *Śrī Tripura Sundarī*

The famous *Sri Vidya* is *Tripurasundari Vidya* only. This is the third one amongst the ten. *Tripurasundari* is the *Icchaa Shakti* (wish energy) of the Supreme Being. The *tantras* do not distinguish the energy and the person who has that energy. Hence *Tripurasundaree*, who is the *Icchaa Shakti* is the Supreme Being. *Upanishats* mention that the knowledge called *Pragnaanam* is energy and hence that is a quality of the Supreme Being. The transcendental form of this *Devi* resides in our forehead between the two eye-brows – the place of *Aagnaa chakra*. This is being conveyed by *Bhālasthā, Indradhanuḥ Prabhā* (*Lalita Sahasranama* 593, 594). The second place is the *Vishuddhi chakra* or *Shanginee Nadi*, the place of dreams, the neck. This is also conveyed by the names *Shiraḥ Sthitā, Chandranibhā* (*Lalita Sahasranama* 591, 592). Thirdly **She** has a place in our hearts – *Hrudayasthā, Raviprakhyā* (*Lalita Sahasranama* 595, 596) – indicating that **She** is in the form of the intellectual who is fond of sleep.

All the three states of a soul (*Jaagrath, Swapna* and *Sushupti* – awakened, sleep and deep sleep states) and the fourth one (*tureeyam* – swoon), which is beyond all these, are all *Tripurasundaree's* only. This *Devi* shines in our body in three places Sun, Moon and fire *mandalas* alongwith the corresponding illumination and hence **She** is called as *Tripurasundaree*. Because of her light the Sun, Moon, fire and lightning get illuminated (*Katopanishat* 2-15).

Vedas convey that only the knowledge of the form of this *Devi* characters the form of Supreme Being – *Satyam* (truth), *Gnana* (knowledge) and *Ananta* (endless) *Brahma* (*Taitreeya Upanishat* 2.1) – so also *Vignanam* (science) and *Ananda* (bliss) *Brahma* (*Brahadaranyaka Upanishat* 39.25).

4. *Śrī Bhuvaneśwarī*

This *Bhuvaneshvaree Devi* indicates the *Gnana Shakti* (knowledge energy) of the Supreme Being. *Tripurasundaree* indicates *icchaa Shakti* (energy of wish) and *Bhairavee* indicates *kriya Shakti* (action energy).

Vedantas say that all the worlds that are known to us are linked as a chain in this ether. Since this ether is *Bhuvaneshvaree* the name most suited to **her** – *Bhuvana* means world and *Eshvaree* means lord or head. **She** has filled herself and protects the world created by **her**. Hence, **she** has the names as *Jagad Dhātrī* (*Lalita Sahasranama* 935) and *Viśvadhārinī* (*Lalita Sahasranama* 759).

Bhuvaneshvaree indicates *Aakash* (ether) *tattva* and *Kaalee* indicates *kala* (time) tattva. *Bhuvaneshvaree* is *Aakash* (ether) *tattva* and *Kaalee* is the sound character (*tanmātra*) originating from it. Hence *Bhuvaneshvaree* acts as a platform for the courageous dance of *Kaalee*. This *Bhuvaneshvaree* shines as *taharaakaasham*, in our heart.

Vedas indicate this *Bhuvaneshvaree* as *Atiti*, spouse of the sage Kashyap. The word Kashyap means one who sees. We have to see the objects only in the ether. This is the story mentioned in *Vedas*.

5.   *Śrī Tripura Bhairavī*

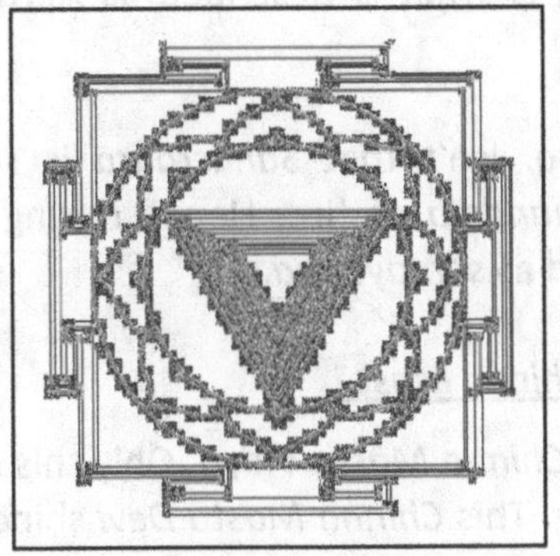 

Out of the ten, the fifth *Bhairavee Vidya* is also called as *Tripura Bhairavee Vidyaa*. **She** resides in the bottom most *Moolaadhaara chakra* in the *Paraa Vaag* (speech) form. The names *Mūlādhāraikanilayā* (*Lalita Sahasranama* 99) and *Vahnimaṇḍalavāsinī* (*Lalita Sahasranama* 352) indicate *Tripura Bhairavī Devi* only. **She** dwells in different places with different names – as *Tripura Bhairavee* in the triangle of fire in *Moolaadhaara* – in the *mandala* of Sun in the heart (*anahata chakra*) as *Bhuvaneshvaree* – as *Tripurasundaree* in *Sasarara* in the 1000 petaled lotus in the *mandala* of Moon. In this *Tripura Bhairavee* indicates *kriya Shakti* (energy of action). Hence the red colour.

According to *Upanishads, Brahma*, in the status of beginning of the creation, was doing penance (thinking). It is mentioned as "*sa tapo tapyata*" (*Taitreeya Upanishat* 2-6). That energy of penance is *Tripura Bhairavee*. Since penance is an action, *Sri Devi* is also called as *kriya Shakti* (energy of action). *Vedas* also pray this *Tripura Bhairavee* as fire or *Durga*, red in colour and shines due to penance (*Durga Sooktam – Rig Veda* 8.7.14).

Tripurasundaree Devi and *Tripurabhairavee Devi* are mutual reflections on account of *Anaahata chakra*. Hence as we have for the mantra of *Tripurasundaree*, we have three halls for this *mantra* also *Vaagbhava, kaamaraaja* and *Shakti koota*. The *Bhairavee*, residing in *Moolaadhaara* will awaken the *kundalinee* and handover to *Sundaree* dwelling in *Sahasraara*. Having satisfied by the nectar called *Sudhaasindu* secreted there, **she** returns to *Moolaadhaara* again. There ordered by *Bhairavee*, goes back to *Sahasraara*. This is what is described as *Aardram jvalati* by the *Sookta*.

This nectar is called *somarasa*. Isn't that *Sahasraara* is *soma mandala*? *Moolaadhaara* is *mandala* of fire. Hence mixing the *somarasa* in the fire is indicated as *somayaaga*.

6.   *Śrī Chinna Mastā*

Out of the ten the sixth one is *Chinna Masta Vidya*. Only this *Devi* is called as *Prachanda Chandee*. This *Chinna Masta Devi* shines in the *Aagnaa chakra* between the two eye brows in our body. Since *Chinna Masta* acts more furious and faster than *Kaalee* **she** is called *Prachanda Chandee*. **She** completes the tasks swiftly without the help of time (*kalam*).

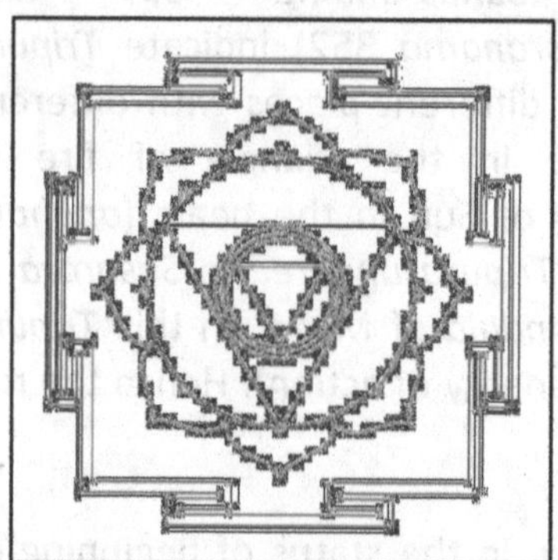

We can compare **her** to the current. Electricity passes into our body so fast through the nerves and completes its activities. Similarly, *Chinna Masta* also spreads the entire body within a second before the eyes wink. The two petals in the *Aagnaa chakra* indicate *icchaa* (wish) and *Gnana* (knowledge). The *Chinna Masta Devi* in that place is also in those forms.

Though there are many *naadis* (pulses) in our body, the 101 *naadis* around the heart are considered as important — "*shadam cha ekaa cha hrudyasya naadyaah*" (*Kaataka Upanishat* 3-2-16). Still important are the three viz., *Idaa, pingala* and *shushumnaa*. *Shushumnaa* is the one which moves in the mid of the spine at the back of our body. *Idaa* and *pingala* coil themselves around both the sides and join the *Shushumnaa* at the *Aagnaa chakra*. This is *Triveni sangama* (meeting of three – as meeting of three rivers Ganga, Yamuna and Saraswathi in Allahabad). *Idaa* is Ganga, *Pingala* – Yamuna and *Shushumnaa* is invisible Saraswathi. This is what is told in *Vedas* as – *"sitaa sito sarito yatra sangate"*.

The energy (*Shakti*) called *atipeekara* running in *Shushumna* is called *Chinna Masta* or *Prachanda Chandee* or *Vajra Virochanee*. *Idaa Varninee Devi* shines like beautiful Moon and **she** carries the nectar. *Daakinee Devi* is in Red colour and shines like Sun. These *Varninee* and *Daakinee Devis* are close aides of *Chinna Masta Devi*.

7. *Śrī Bhagalāmukhī*

Bagalaamukhee is the eighth *Vidya* among the ten. This *Devi* has other names like *Peetaambaraa* or *Dhandanaathaa*. People used to worship this *Devi*, mainly to win over the enemies and to win over others in debates. However, this *Devi* is capable of providing all the four wishes (beneficence, worldly substances, happiness and bliss). A book called *Sri Bagalaamukhee Rahasya* published by *Sri Peetaambara Peeta* in a place called *Dadiya* in Madhya Pradesh, India, clearly deals in detail about the worshipping methods of this *Devi* and its results with evidences.

Bagalaamukhee Devi is the one who protected Lord *Parameswara* from the demon *Basmaasura*. **She** also protected Lord *Narayana*, who was in the form of a child in *Vadabadra*. **She** removes all the sorrows of her devotees. **She** is the remover of enemies.

The word *bagaalaa* is the transformation from the Samskruta word *valkaa*. *Valkaa* means bridle. *Valka* transformed into *Vaklaa* and then to *Bagaalaa*. Such a transformation has been seen in the words like *simha – himsa, pashyaka – kashyapa*. A bridle controls the mouth of a horse. Similarly worship of this *Devi* controls the mouth and other organs of an enemy. A very important letter of *Bagalaamukhee mantra* is *Hrleem*.

8. <u>*Śrī Dhūmāvatī*</u>

 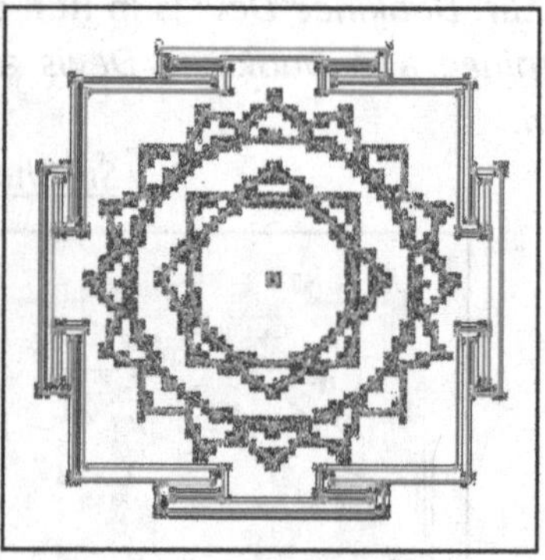

Dhoomaavatee Devi is the seventh among the ten. In *tantra shaastras* the word energy will always indicate one with that energy. *Kali* to *Kalee*, *Akshobya* to *Tara* and *Bhairava* to *Bhairavee*. But *Dhoomaavatee* is taking a deviation to this convention. Hence *tantras* mention that **she** is spouseless. *Dhoomaavatee Devi* indicates smoke, darkness and innocence. But when there is a smoke there should be fire. The concepts dark and innocence hide light and wisdom. Hence with the blessings of *Dhoomaavatee Devi* we can easily reach knowledge by removing the darkness of innocence and by destroying the enemies like obstructions, who are friends of darkness. This is the essence of *Dhoomaavatee Vidyaa*. That is the reason, the important result of *Dhoomaavatee Vidyaa* is destruction of enemies. As mentioned earlier, enemies are within ourselves. Once the enemies of knowledge namely suspicion and diversity have been uprooted, the blessings of the *guru* through belief and devotion and the liberation can easily be reached through the knowledge of *Brahmam*.

When *Daskhayani* fired herself in the fire of the *yagna*, this *Dhoomaavatee* originated from the smoke of the fire and hence this name (*Dhooma* = smoke). **She** has crow in her flag and in some places, **she** sits on a crow.

The *mantra* and the process of worshipping *Dhoomaavatee* has been clearly explained in *Bhetkaarinee tantra*. It is seen there that this *mantra* will result in destroying the enemies – "*Dhoomaavatee Manuḥ prokto vairi vigraha karakaḥ*" The golden voice of *Meru Tantra* is that the devotee who worships this *Mahaavidyaa*, which has eight letters, can get complete attainment.

9. *Śrī Mātangī*

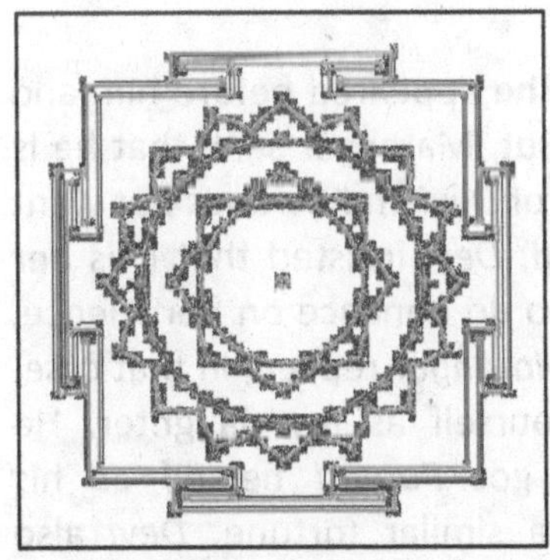 

Matangi is the ninth *Vidyaa* among the ten. **She** is a minister of *Sri Lalita Devi*. The important activity of ours in this world is speech. This is also called as sound or *vaag*. One of the important energies that support this activity is *Matangi Devi*. This speech has four stages viz., *Paraa*, *Pashyanti*, *Madhyamaa* and *Vaikharee*. It has already been seen that, out of these, *Tripurabhairavee* is in the form of *Paraa Vaag* and *Tara Devi* in the form of *Pashyanti*. *Vaikharee vaag* is the last stage among these. The *Paraa*, which is stationed in *Moolaadhaara*, becomes *Pashyanti* when it moves to *Manipooraka chakra*. Again, when it is move out it turns as *Vaikharee* in *Vishuddhi chakra* in neck. *Matangi* is in this form of *Vaikharee*.

This *Matangi Devi* is also called *Ucchishta Chaandaalee*, *Raaja Matangi* or *Shyaamalaa*. *Shyaamalaa* means black object. *Shaastras* indicate the pure sound, at the moment when it indicates an object in this world, as black. Hence it is also called as *Chaandaalee*. This stage is the last one in speech and hence indicated as the last caste as a simile.

During the *Makara* month (Jan-Feb), *Shyaamalaa Navaratri* is being celebrated by *Shakta* devotees.
One of the tribes living in Yaazhpaanam in Sri Lanka is called Matangar. One of the sages borne in this tribe was called as *Matanga Muni*. In Ramayana, we have heard of Sabari, an old lady, waiting for *Sri* Rama and offered him fruits after tasting herself. This *Matanga Muni* was the guru of Sabari. His father was a *Sri Vidyaa Upasaka*. *Matanga Muni* got initiated into *Sri Vidyaa* from his father himself.

He did heavy penance on *Sri Devi*. **She** appeared before him and asked what is the boon he wants. But, Matangar said, that he is happy with the very sight (*darshan*) of *Devi* and he does not want any other boon. On the other hand, *Devi* insisted that it is **her** practice to offer boons to those who do penance on **her**. Hence, **she** has to give some boon to him. *Matangar* replied, in that case, give me the fortune of having yourself as my daughter. He remembered his friend Himavan got *Parvati* herself as his daughter. Matangar also wanted a similar fortune. *Devi* also agreed. Thus, born *Shyaamalaa Devi* to the parents *Matangar* and *Siddhimati*. Being daughter of *Matangar*, she is called as *Matangi*. Being an incarnation of *Shyamala*, she is also called as *Rajashyamala* or *Raja Matangi*. In Samskrutam, *shyaamaa* means a mix of blue and green colours. In North India this *Devi* is called as *Shyaamaa*.

In *Shakta* worship, we have 7 forms of *Devi* called *Sapta Mata*-s. *Shyaamalaa* is one among them. Others being – *Brahmi*, *Maheshwari*, *Koumari*, *Indrani* (*Aindri*), *Chamundi* and *Varahi*.

Matangi alias *Shyamala Devi* appears both in the list of *Sapta Mata*-s and *Dasha Maha Vidya* as well.

Kalidas's Shyaamalaa Dandakam goes this way –

Mātā Maragata Śyāmā Mātangī Madaśālinī ----
Mātanga Kanyām Manasā Smarāmi.

His other works like *Raghuvamsa, Kumara Sambavam, Mega Santesham*, etc., are very famous. *Kalidas* was so innocent and ignorant, but he became the greatest poet in Samskrutam. All these are possible only because of the blessings of *Matangi*. The idol worshipped by *Kalidas* can still be seen at Ujjain. There are two *Sahasranama*-s about this *Devi* – *Shyamala Sahasranama* and *Raja Matangi Sahasranama*.

A story goes in *Mahabharata* written by *Vyasa* – *Devi* incarnated as a daughter of a sage called *Matanga*, who is a *chandaala*, a low caste person. Hence her name *Chandaalee*. *Mati* means mind. *Matam* means thought. *Matanga* means the status of explaining the thought. When it explains the sound, it becomes *Matangi*. This is the tattva of *Matangi*. Even when this transforms to many states, the base form as *Paraavaag* in the *Moolaadhaara* energy does not get destructed. That is eternal. That always remains as residue. That is the reason **she** is called as *Uchchishta Chaandaalee* or *Shyaamalaa* since, **she** acts as a guide to reach the residual *Paraavaag* and since **she** is in the circumstance to indicate the original objects of this world.

There is one more story about the incarnation of *Matangi Devi* – this story is mentioned in the *Tiruvenkaadu Stalapuranam*.

During one of the dissolution periods, *Brahma* in the form of an elephant was on a meditation on *Lord Shiva*. At that time, a son was born from the minds of *Brahma*. He is *Matangar* (*matanga* means elephant). Brahma ordered Matangar to perform penance. Since it was the dissolution period, the entire universe was flooded. Sage Narada came to him and suggested that even during dissolution period the Tiruvenkaadu is not flooded and he can go and do penance at that place. Matangar was happy and started his penance at Tiruvenkaadu. *Manmata* (Cupid) tried to disturb his penance. *Lord Shiva* burnt him into ashes through his third eye. Lord *Vishnu* disguising as *Mohini*, a beautiful lady appeared before Matangar. He requested Vishnu to stay at Tiruvenkaadu as Mohini and Vishnu also accepted. Being happy about the penance of Matangar, Lord Ganesh visited him and offered eight *siddhis* (*ashta siddhis*). At last Lord Shiva also appeared before Matangar and blessed.

As per the request of Matangar, Shyamala *Devi* incarnated as a baby girl in a Bloom (*Neelotbala*) flower, in the Matanga pond in the early mornings of a Friday of *Aashaadha* month (Jul-Aug). Matangar brought this girl and grew her. Still there is one *Matanga Ashrama* (hermitage of sage Matangar) 3 KMs from Tiruvenkaadu village.

10. *Śrī Kamalātmikā*

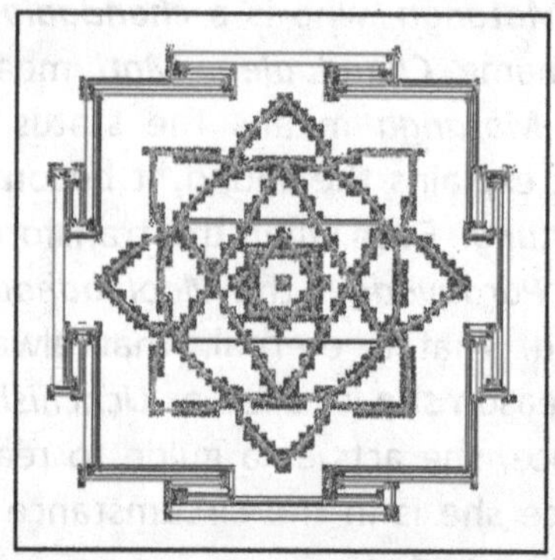

This is the last *Vidya* among the ten. This is also called as *Sri Vidya*. The *Vidya* of *Sundari* is called as *panchadhashee*. It has 15 letters. If one more letter is added to *panchadhashee* it becomes *shodashee vidya*. This is *Kamalatmika's*.

Kamala means lotus. This *Devi* sits on a lotus flower. **She** is praised in *puranas* as *Mahalakshmi*, consort of Lord *Vishnu*, holding lotus flowers in both **her** hands. Everyone in this world seek **her** compassion.

The status before the creation of this world is called the status of

Dhoomavatee. After the creation, when it stabilises it is called as the status of *Kamalatmikaa*. The beauty in every field of this globe is only due to **her**. The 15 *Rigs* in *Rig Veda* (*Sri Sookta*) describe **her** in detail. This *Sookta* is part of *Veda* used by every worshipper of *Devi*. With the compassion of this *Devi* the devotee becomes expert in all fields.

There are *Ashtotra* and *Sahasranamas* available on this *Devi*. *Sri* Muthusamy Deekshitar also has sung *Navaavarna* songs on Kamala *Devi*. She is very fond of bestowing boons to her devotees.

If the blessings of this Devi go out of any person or thing, then he/it becomes useless and becomes averse to others.

Thus, Dashavatar of *Sri Devi* brings in various health, wealth and blessings to the devotees in this world and also the liberation (Moksha) in the other world by compassion of Ambikai.

*****

Seven Mothers

People worship *Śrī Devī* in various forms like, Seven Mothers (*Sapta Mātās*), *Sapta Kannikās*, *Nava Durgā*[18], *Dasha Mahā Vidyā* and so on. In villages *Sapta Mātās* are used to be called as *Kannimār*. They are also called as *Kātthāyi*, *Karumāri*, *Mahamayi* and so on. Most of the *Devī* temples and even some *Śiva* temples have the idols of *Sapta Mātās*. Various texts like *Devī Bhagavatam*, *Devī Puranam*, *Mārkaṇḍeya Puranam*, *Vamana Puranam*, *Vishnu Dharmottaram*, *Mahākāli Māhātmyam* and so on so forth, describe about *Sapta Mātās*.

In the *Mahabharata*, Lord *Krishna* went as a messenger of *Pandavas* to the palace of *Drudarashtran*. At that time, he showed his *Vishvaroopam*. It is hailed that people could see the forms of *Sapta Mātās* in the *Vishvaroopa* body of Lord *Krishna*.

The names of *Sapta Mātās* are – *Brāhmī*, *Maheśvarī*, *Koumārī*, *Vaiṣṇavī*, *Vārāhī*, *Aindrī* and *Cāmuṇḍī*. The story of their incarnations has been mentioned differently in various scripts.

Just before the killing of the demon *Antakāsura*, Lord *Śiva* was in *Yoga nidra*. *Antakāsura* tried to attack *Pārvati*. Immediately *Pārvati* thought of *Brahmā*, *Viṣṇu* and other *devas*. When *Pārvati*, as a lady was alone, devas did not want to help her in the male form and hence they took the female forms as;

1. The *Shakti* of *Brahmā* as *Brāhmī*,
2. The *Shakti* of *Maheṣvaran* as *Maheśvarī*,
3. The *Shakti* of *Kumaran* as *Koumārī*,
4. The *Shakti* of *Viṣṇu* as *Vaiṣṇavī*,
5. The *Shakti* of *Anantan* as *Vārāhī*. In some schools, it is also mentioned as the *Shakti* of the Goddess Earth.
6. The *Shakti* of *Indran* as *Aindrī*
7. The *Shakti* of *Eṣānar* as *Cāmuṇḍī*.

---

[18] *Śrī Devī Kavacam* details about *Nava Durgā*.

Lots of sub-*Shaktis* to the above *Devīs* also were formed from different *Devas*. *Pārvati Devī* ordered all these *Devīs* to fight with *Antakāsura*. When they were fighting, Lord *Śiva* waked up from *Yoga nidra* and stabbed *Antakāsura* with his trident. He sought the apology of Lord *Śiva* and *Pārvati Devī* while hanging from the trident. Lord *Śiva*, called as *Āśutoṣi*[19] forgave and made him the head of one of the *Gaṇas*. This incident has happened in *Tirukoilur* and that has been mentioned in that *Stala Puraṇam*.

Another story is mentioned in *Mārkaṇdeya Puranam* – To assassinate *Mahiṣāsura*, *Śrī Devī* took the form of *Durgā*, as an integrated *Shakti* of all the *Devas* like *Brahmā*, *Viṣṇu*, *Indra* and various other *Devas*. Demons *Caṇḍa* and *Munḍa* frowned at the beauty of *Śrī Devī* wanted to marry **her**. They sent a messenger called *Sugrīvan*. This story is mentioned in *Śrī Devī Māhātmyam*. *Śrī Devī* with anger created various forms from different organs of her body like;

1.   *Brāhmī* from face
2.   *Maheśvarī* from naval
3.   *Koumārī* from neck
4.   *Vaiṣṇavī* from hands
5.   *Vārāhī* from back
6.   *Aindrī* from breasts
7.   *Cāmuṇḍī* from forehead.

With the help of these *Devīs*, *Śrī Sarasvati Devi*, destroyed the demons *Caṇḍa* and *Munḍa*. These seven mothers got the boon of remaining at the first *Āvaraṇam* of *Śrī Chakram* called as *Trailokya Mohana Chakram*. They serve *Śrī Lalitā Devī* from here and bless the worshippers. Let us try to learn something about all these *Devīs* individually;

<u>1.   *Brāhmī*;</u>

Among the three Gods (*Trimūrtis*), *Brahmā* is the first one. His task precedes others'. After he creating the creatures other two

---

[19] The meaning of *Āśutoṣi* is – giver of anything sought for.

Gods can protect and destroy. In the same way *Brāhmī* is the first Goddess among the seven. He is the feature of *Brahmā*. Her vehicle is swan. She protects everything in the west direction. She wears the skin of spotted deer as her dress. Worshipping *Brahmā* is related to worshipping Sun. Hence, it is told as, *Sandyā Devī* herself is in this form. She spreads the Sun rays, has four heads like *Brahmā*, has *Kamaṇḍalu*, Rosary, Books, etc., in her hand. While fighting she display herself with weapons in hand. This *Devi's*;

- *Bījā* (root) *mantra – 'Brām'*
- *Mantra – Oṃ Brām Brāhmyai Namaḥ*
- *Gāyatrī – Oṃ Brahma Śaktyai Ca Vidmahe Pītavarṇayai Ca Dīmahe Tanno Brāhmī Pracodayāt.*

2. Maheśvarī;

She blesses us sitting on a bull as a feature of Lord *Śivā* called as *Maheśvaran*. She has a Deer, an axe, a knife, a skull, safe and boon signet hands and five faces. She has an eye on the forehead and a crescent on the head. With all these she protects all of us. She is amidst and feel happy among the sages and *Veda* chanting of groups of *Nandis*. Demon *Mahiśāsura* was killed by her trident

only. 'Maha' means yagna. Only when the yagnas are properly and abundantly performed rain will not fail and the country will prospect. She is the protector of such yagnas.

This *Devi's*;

- Colour is white
- *Bījā* (root) *mantra – 'Mām'*
- *Mantra – Oṃ Mām Māheśvaryai Namaḥ*

- *Gāyatrī – Oṃ Śveta Varṇāyai Ca Vidmahe Śūla Hastāyai Ca Dīmahe Tanno Maheśvarī Pracodayāt.*

3. *Koumārī;*

Koumārī is the feature of *Kumāran*, son of Lord *Śiva*. Her vehicle is peacock. She has other names like *Şaşţi Devi*, *Devasenā* and so on. She has six heads; twelve hands and she hold a divine spear and leads the army. She originated from the neck of *Śrī Devī*. She bestows children.

This *Devi's*;

- Colour is red
- *Bījā* (root) *mantra – 'Goum'*
- *Mantra – Oṃ Goum Koumāryai Namaḥ*
- *Gāyatrī – Oṃ Śikhi Vāhanāyai Ca Vidmahe Shakti Hastāyai Ca Dīmahe Tanno Koumārī Pracodayāt.*

4. *Vaiṣṇavī;*

Vaiṣṇavī is a feature of *Mahāviṣṇu* and originated from the hands of *Parāśakti*. Religions texts do indicate that male form of *Parāśakti* is *Viṣṇu*. In most of the places it has been mentioned that *Viṣṇu's* sister is *Parāśakti*. In the form of *Śaṅkara Nārāyaṇa*, the left half of *Śiva* is *Viṣṇu*. In the form of *Arddhanārīśvara*[20], the left half of *Śiva* is *Parāśakti*. What does this indicate? *Viṣṇu* and *Parāśakti* are one and the same. The sentence, "*Bhokeca Bhavāni, Puruşeca Viṣṇu, Krodeca Kāli, Samareca Durgā*" is worth comparable in this context. The

---

[20] 392nd name in *Śrī Lalitā Sahasranāma – Śrīkaṇṭhārdhaśarīriṇī* - श्रीकण्ठार्धशरीरिणी

protecting Goddess *Mahālakśmi*, in the form of *Vaiṣṇavī* sits on an Eagle (*Garuda*), with a peaceful face, with conch and chakra in the hands, bestows all wealth, health and all to her devotees.

This *Devi's*;

- Colour is white
- *Bījā* (root) *mantra* – 'Vaim'
- *Mantra* – *Oṃ Vaim Vaiṣṇavyai Namaḥ*
- *Gāyatrī* – *Oṃ Śyāma Varṇāyai Ca Vidmahe Chakra Hastāyai Ca Dīmahe Tanno Vaiṣṇavī Pracodayāt.*

5. *Vārāhī*;

Vārāhī originated from the back portion of *Parāśakti* and is a feature of *Anantan*. Some schools opine that she is a feature of the Goddess Earth and some say that she is a feature *Vārāha* incarnation of lord *Viṣṇu*. In a way these two are connected, since during *Vārāha* incarnation, lord *Viṣṇu* married Goddess Earth. She has a face of a boar. She is the knight of the army of *Parāśakti*. She is called by other names like *Pañcami, Daṇḍini, Daṇḍanāthā* and so on.

During the battle with *Tārukāsuran*, she was the chief of army for *Kāli*. During the battle with *Sumbāsuran*, she was the chief of army for *Caṇḍī Devī*. During the battle with *Baṇḍāsuran*, she was the chief of army for *Śrī Lalitā Devī*. Her chariot is called *Giri Chakram*. She has a hull in her hand. The statement "*Vārāhī Vīrya Nandanā*" means – she is full of velour, fire and anger. There used to be a saying that "don't argue with the devotee of *Vārāhī*. She has various vehicles like Lion, Deer, Snake, etc. The nine days during month of *Āḍi* (July-August) is celebrated as "*Vārāhi Navarāthri*".

This *Devi's*;

- Colour is black

- *Bījā* (root) *mantra – 'Vām'*
- *Mantra – Oṃ Vām Vārāhyai Namaḥ*
- *Gāyatrī – Oṃ Śyāmalāyai Ca Vidmahe Hala Hastāyai Ca Dīmahe Tanno Vārāhī Pracodayāt.*

6. <u>Aindrī;</u>

Only if a person has performed 1000 *Aśvameda yagnas*, he is eligible to become the post of *Indran*. He is the head of 300 crores of *Devas* and *Aṣṭa Dik Bālās. Aindrī* is a feature of such an Indran and originated from the breast portion of *Parāśakti*. Hence, she has that *Irāvata* elephant itself as her vehicle. She has *Kulicam* and Thunder Bolt (*Vajrāyutam*) in her hands. She bestows beauty, courage and rich life to her devotees. She is indicated as *Indrāṇi.*

This *Devi's*;

- Colour is Indra Blue stone. In some places it is also mentioned as white.
- *Bījā* (root) *mantra – 'Īm'*
- *Mantra – Oṃ Īm Aindriyai Namaḥ*
- *Gāyatrī – Oṃ Śyāma Varṇāyai Ca Vidmahe Vajra Hastāyai Ca Dīmahe Tanno Aindrī Pracodayāt.*

7. <u>Cāmuṇḍī;</u>

Cāmuṇḍī originated from the forehead of *Parāśakti* and is a feature of *Īśānan*. According to *Śrī Devī Mahatmyam*, she destroyed the demons like

Caṇḍan and *Muṇḍan* and hence this name. In the state Karnataka, *Śrī Devī* is worshipped in the name of *Cāmuṇḍī*. In Mysore there is a world-famous temple for *Cāmuṇḍī*. In various villages there are deities called *Cāmuṇḍī*. She has a corpse as her vehicle. She is red in colour and courageous and hence bestows success to her devotees.

This *Devi's*;

- Colour is black. In some places it has been mentioned as Red.
- *Bījā* (root) *mantra – 'Cām'*
- *Mantra – Oṃ Cām Cāmuṇḍāyai Namaḥ*
- *Gāyatrī – Oṃ Kriṣṇa Varṇāyai Ca Vidmahe Śula Hastāyai Ca Dīmahe Tanno Cāmuṇḍī Pracodayāt.*

<u>Seven Mothers – a summary</u>;

A demon called *Tārukan*, did deep penance with *Brahmā* and he got a boon of immortality. He also got the strength of *Amruta* and *Brahma Daṇḍam* and hence he was roaming with ego. He installed his kingdom in the world of *Devas* and harassed *Devas*. *Devas* prayed with *Brahmā* and he cursed *Tārukan* that he would be destroyed by a lady. All *Devas*, including *Brahmā*, *Viṣṇu*, *Rudra* and all prayed *Śrī Devī*. Seven Mothers originated from her as described earlier. *Maheśvari* stabbed *Tārukan* and from his blood, lot many demons originated. *Tārukan* trumpeted Lord *Śiva*. *Badra Kāli* originated from Lord *Śiva*'s third eye on the forehead. Her image was so scary that *Pārvati* herself was terrified. On *Pārvati*'s request *Badra Kāli* reduced to somewhat peaceful image with 3 eyes and 16 hands. She drank all the blood oozing from the body of *Tārukan* and killed him alongwith seven Mothers.

We have separate temples for seven Mothers in many a place. In some temples, there is separate shrines. Some worth noting are – Seven Mothers temple at Karuppur near Jeeyapuram at Trichy, Tamilnadu. There is a special shrine for seven Mothers in the *Māngādu* temple at Chennai in the west behind the main deity. There is another temple seven mother at *Vālāḍi* village near Trichy.

Let us worship seven mothers and get all types of blessings.

<u>Seven Mothers – at a glance;</u>

Mother	*Śakti*	Originated from (organ)	Colour	*Bījam*	*Mantram*	*Gāyatrī*
Brāhmī	Brahmā	Face		Brām	Om Brām Brāhmyai Nama	Om Brahma Śaktyai Ca Vidmahe Pītavarṇayai Ca Dīmahe Tanno Brāhmī Pracodayāt
Maheśvarī	Maheśvaran	Naval	White	Mām	Om Mām Māheśvaryai Nama	Om Śveta Varṇāyai Ca Vidmahe Śūla Hastāyai Ca Dīmahe Tanno Maheśvarī Pracodayāt
Koumārī	Kumāran	Neck	Red	Goum	Om Goum Koumāryai Nama	Om Śikhi Vāhanāyai Ca Vidmahe Shakti Hastāyai Ca Dīmahe Tanno Koumārī Pracodayāt
Vaiṣṇavī	Viṣṇu	Hands	White	Vaim	Om Vaim Vaiṣṇavyai Nama	Om Śyāma Varṇāyai Ca Vidmahe Chakra Hastāyai Ca Dīmahe Tanno Vaiṣṇavī Pracodayāt

Mother	Śakti	Originated from (organ)	Colour	Bījam	Mantram	Gāyatrī
Vārāhī	Anantan or Goddess Earth	Back	Black	*Vām*	*Om Vām Vārāhyai Nama*	*Om Śyāmalāyai Ca Vidmahe Hala Hastāyai Ca Dīmahe Tanno Vārāhī Pracodayāt*
Aindrī	Indran	Breast	Indra Blue stone or white	*Īm*	*Om Īm Aindriyai Nama*	*Om Śyāma Varṇāyai Ca Vidmahe Vajra Hastāyai Ca Dīmahe Tanno Aindrī Pracodayāt*
Cāmuṇḍī	Īśānan	Forehead	Black/ red	*Cām*	*Om Cām Cāmuṇḍyai Nama*	*Om Kriṣṇa Varṇāyai Ca Vidmahe Śula Hastāyai Ca Dīmahe Tanno Cāmuṇḍī Pracodayāt*

*****

Titi Nityā Devīs

In the *Śrī Chakra*, around the *Bindu*, on each of the three sides of the triangle, 5 *Nityā Devis* are sitting – totally 15 *Nityā Devis*. They are immortal and identify the time. They are respectively – *Kameśvari, Bagamālini, Nityaklinnā, Beruṇḍā, Vahnivāsinī, Mahā Vajreśvari, Śivadhūti, Tvaritā, Kulasundarī, Nityā, Nīlapatākā, Vijayā, Sarvamaṅgalā, Jvālāmālinī* and *Chitrā*. At the center *Śrī Devī* herself decorate the *Bindu* as 16th *Mahā Nityā Devi*.

These 16 *Nityā Devis* alongwith *Śyāmalā* and *Vārāhi* stand protecting the *Śrī Chakra*.

Mātaḥ Maho Tayite Lalite Hayāsya Kumbodbhavāti Sannuta

Divya Kīrtte

Kāmeśvari Prakruti Titi Devatāpiḥ Samsevitāṅgri Yugaḷe ||

The summary meaning of the above verse is – Enchanting beautiful, without leaving Lord *Śivā*, adored by scholars like *Hayagrīva, Agastya* and all, shining in the center of the *Śrī Chakra*, starting from the bottom of the triangle in the anticlockwise worshipped as 15 *Titi Nityā Devis*, viz., *Kameśvari, Bagamālini* and so on. Our humble *pranāms* to her.

These 15 *Nityās* represent 15 *titis* and hence they are called as *Titi Nityās*. During bright lunar fortnight from *Pratama* till *Pourṇami* (full moon) – from *Kameśvari* to *Chitrā*. During dark lunar fortnight from *Pratama* till *Amāvāsya* (new

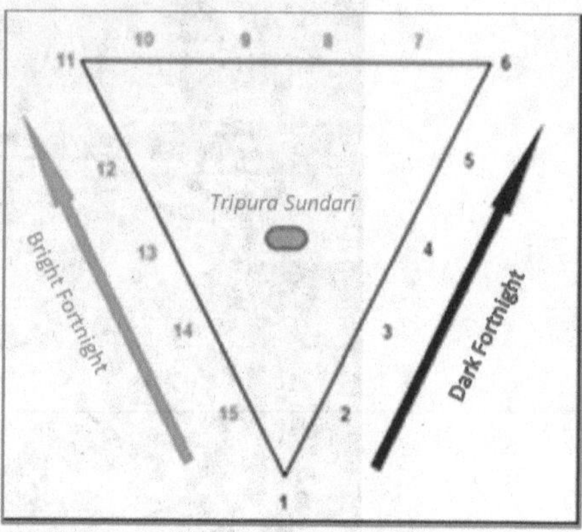

moon) – from *Chitrā* to *Kameśvari*. 16th *Nityā Devī* is *Parāśakti* herself.

#	Nityā Devī	Crescent Moon	Bright Lunar Fortnight	Dark Lunar Fortnight
1.	Kameśvari	Amrutakalā	Pratamai	New Moon
2.	Bagamālini	Mānatā	Dvitiyai	Caturdaśi
3.	Nityaklinnā	Pūṣā	Tritiyai	Trayodaśi
4.	Beruṇḍā	Tuṣṭi	Caturtti	Dvādaśi
5.	Vahnivāsinī	Puṣṭi	Pañcami	Ekādaśi
6.	Mahā Vajreśvari	Rati	Śaṣṭi	Daśami
7.	Śivadhūti	Truti	Saptami	Navami
8.	Tvaritā	Cacini	Aṣṭami	Aṣṭami
9.	Kulasundarī	Candrikā	Navami	Saptami
10.	Nityā	Śānti	Daśami	Śaṣṭi
11.	Nīlapatākā	Jyotsnā	Ekādaśi	Pañcami
12.	Vijayā	Śrīkalā	Dvādaśi	Caturtti
13.	Sarvamaṅgalā	Prīti	Trayodaśi	Tritiyai
14.	Jvālāmālinī	Angatā	Caturdaśi	Dvitiyai
15.	Chitrā	Pūrṇā	Full Moon	Pratamai
16.	Mahā Nityā	Pūrṇāmruta Sāgarā	Parāśakti, the paradise always shining with 16 crescents.	

There are crescent moons optimally pertaining to each of the *Titi Nityā Devīs*, because the facial region of *Śrī Lalitā Devī* shines like a full Moon 16 crescents integrated within.

Each of the 15 letters of *Pañcadaśākśarī mantra* pertain to each of the 15 *Titi Nityā Devīs*. Hence *Pañcadaśākśarī mantra* and *Titi Nityās* are synonyms. All causal of the soul is *Mahānityai*.

Each of the *Nityās* is in *Prakāśa*[21] form during day time and *Vimarśa* form during night. They are also in the form of time and hence they are call *Kāla Atiṣṭāna Devīs*.

It is evident from the names in *Śrī Lalitā Sahasranāma*, that *Śrī Lalitā Devī* herself is in the forms of each of the *Nityā Devīs*.

#	*Nityā Devī*	# in *Lalitā Sahasranāma*	Name in *Lalitā Sahasranāma*
1.	Kameśvari	33, 77, 82, 373	Various names
2.	Bagamālini	277	Bagamālini
3.	Nityaklinnā	388	Nityaklinnā
5.	Vahnivāsinī	352	Vahni Maṇḍala Vāsinī
6.	Mahā Vajreśvari	468	Vajreśvari
7.	Śivadhūti	405	Śivadhūti
10.	Nityā	136	Nityā
12.	Vijayā	346	Vijayā
13.	Sarvamaṅgalā	200	Sarvamaṅgalā
14.	Jvālāmālinī	71	Jvālāmālinīkakśipta Vahni Prākāra Madyagā

In the tradition of *Śrī Vidyā*, worshipping *Titi Nityā Devis* is an important part. We saw that *Śrī Devī* herself is in the form of all these *Nityā Devis*. She herself takes the role of 16th *Nityā Devi*, called *Mahā Nityā Devi*.

---

[21] *Prakāśa* and *Vimarśa*, the Light of Consciousness and the Power of Self-Awareness respectively

The text called *"Tantra Rāja Tantrum"* describes about *Nityā Devis* in detail. It has been mentioned that *Titi Nityā Devis* are connected subtle sound originations. They are in the form of time alongwith 36 philosophies. They are the vowels in Samskruta language. They are the universe. One Year has 360 days and 360 nights (totaling 720). There are 720 aspects of *Devis* in a year. Each *Devi* rules 100 *Nāḍis* in our body. Our body has 72,000 *Nāḍis*. The full circle of the *Nityās* also represents the 21,600 breaths a human being takes in a full day and night.

Other *Śāstra* texts mention that they are integrated with the five base elements like ether, air, etc. They are the 15 letters of *Pañcadaśākśarī mantra*. They are the bright lunar fortnights, as the names given in Vedas – *Darśā, Druṣṭā*[22], etc.

The book *Tantra Rāja Tantrum*, explains pooja methods alongwith meditation verses and all, individually for each of these *Titi Nityā Devis*. The meditation verses and the images may vary depending on the wish and request of the worshipper. The philosophy that these *Titi Nityā Devis* and the *Śrī Chakram* are integrated, is *Meru Prastāram*.

It has been mentioned in various places in *Śrī Lalitā Sahasranāmam* about *Titi Nityā Devis*. *Śrī Bhāskararāyar*, in his *Bhāṣyam*, explains;

73rd name – *Nityāparākramāṭopa Nirīkśaṇa Samutsukā* – नित्या पराक्रमाटोप निरीक्षण समुत्सुका;

Once in the course of the battle with *Bhaṇḍasura*, two of his generals *Damanaka* and *Chitragupta* surrounded the *Śrī Chakrarāja* chariot and started waging a war by unfair means; at that time the 15 *Titi Nityā Devis* proved their prowess by destroying them in front of *Śrī Devī*, much to **Her** delight. **She** was enthused by the *Nitya Devi's* celebrating the invasion of the enemy's army.

Because of their permanence (immortality), the *Ātma Śaktis* (the

---

[22] These names are listed elsewhere in this chapter

soul) are called *Nityās*. *Parākramāṭopa* – growing due to inward self-realization. One who is pleased with that. A person attains external bliss when the immortal soul power wins over the demonic forces, which raise their head from time to time within the mind.

391st name – *Nityā Ṣoḍhaśikārūpā* – निल्या षोढशिकारूपा;

The 15 titis and names accordingly *Śākta* and *Veda*[23] tradition are;

Śākta Veda Tradition	Bright lunar fortnight		Dark lunar fortnight	
	Days	**Nights**	**Days**	**Nights**
Kāmeśwarī	*Samgnānam*	*Darṣā*	*Prastutam*	*Sudhā*
Bagamālinī	*Vignanām*	*Druṣṭā*	*Viśtutam*	*Sunvatī*
Nityaklinnā	*Pragnānam*	*Darśatā*	*Samstutam*	*Prasūtā*
Beruṇḍā	*Jānat*	*Viṣvarūpā*	*Kalyānam*	*Sūyamānā*
Vahnivāsinī	*Abhinānat*	*Sudarṣanā*	*Viṣvarūpā*	*Abhiśūyamānā*
Mahāvajreśwarī	*Sankalpamānam*	*Āpyāyamānām*	*Sūkram*	*Bhītī*
Śivadūtī	*Prakalpamānam*	*Pyāyamānam*	*Amrutam*	*Prabhā*
Twaritā	*Upakalpamānam*	*Āpyāyā*	*Teśavi*	*Śambhā*
Kulasundarī	*Upakluptam*	*Sunrutā*	*Tehaḥ*	*Trupti*
Nityā	*Kluptam*	*Irā*	*Samittam*	*Tarpayantī*
Nīlapatākā	*Sreyaḥ*	*Āpūryamānā*	*Aruṇam*	*Kāntā*
Vijayā	*Vasīyaḥ*	*Pūryamānā*	*Bānumat*	*Kāmyā*
Sarvamaṅgalā	*Āyat*	*Pūrāyantī*	*Marīchimat*	*Kāmajātā*
Jvālāmālinī	*Sambūtam*	*Pūrṇā*	*Abitapat*	*Āyushmatī*
Chitrā	*Būtam*	*Pourṇamāsī*	*Tapasvat*	*Kāmadukā*

We have presiding deities for the 15 days from first to full moon day. They are all the limbs of *Śrī Devī*. *Śrī Devī* herself is the

---

[23] These names can be observed during annual *Upākarma*, at the start of *Vedas*.

sixteenth *Nityā* – i.e. *Mahānityā*. **She** is also called as *Sādākya Kalā*. The description, method of *pooja*, *mantra*, *yantra*, etc., are described in detail in *Tantra Rāja Tantra*.

We are aware that the, according to *Vedas*, bright lunar fortnight has been divided in three parts viz. 5, 6 and 4. This indicates the 3 *kūṭas* in the *Pañcadaśī mantra*.

These *Titi Nityās* are worshipped from *Kāmeshwarī* to *Chitra* during bright lunar fortnight and from *Chitra* to *Kāmeshwarī* during dark lunar fortnight.

These *Titi Nityās Devīs* indicate that *Śrī Devī* is in the form of era. *Bāvano Upaniṣat* advises as; "*Pancadaśa Titirūpeṇa Kālasya Pariṇāma Valokanam.*

During the bright lunar fortnight, the Moon grows by absorbing the rays of the Sun. During dark lunar fortnight the brightness of the Moon decreases step by step. The *Titi Nityās* are also in this form.

For further reading about *Titi Nityās*, the book *Tantra Rāja Tantrum* and/ or the *Lakśmīdhara's* explanation for the 32ⁿᵈ verse of *Soundaryalaharī* can be referred.

<u>610ᵗʰ name</u> – *Pratipan Mukhyarākānta Titimaṇḍalapūjitā* – प्रतिपन्मुख्यारा कान्त तिथिमण्डलपूजिता;

Pratipat means *Pratama*, the first day. *Rākā* means full Moon. She is being worshipped in all these fifteen days. The *Veda* names given in the above table, for each of the fifteen days. Above all these there is a *kala* called *Sādā* in the galaxy of Moon (*Candramaṇḍala*). All these sixteen are called *Titimaṇḍala*.

Titinityā Yajanam is an important part of *Śrī Vidyā* worship. It has been mentioned in *Varāha Purāṇa* that *Agni* (fire) and other gods are the presiding deities for all these *Tities*.

<u>775ᵗʰ name</u> – *Merunilayā* – मेरुनिलया;

According to the saying; *Meruḥ Sumeruḥ Hemādriḥ – Meru* is a golden mountain. It can be reminded that this was mentioned in the 55th name *Sumeru Madhya Sruñggastā*. It is said that *Śrī Devī*'s *Chintāmaṇi* house is at the top of the center peak.

After the demolition of the demon *Bhaṇḍāsura*, *Devas* ordered their architect *Viśvakarma* and the architect of demons *Mayan*, to construct an appropriate place for *Kāmeśwarā* and *Kāmeśwarī*. It was the *Deva's* wish that in the ocean called *Nitya Gnānam* in the midst of 16 *kṣetrās*, *Śrī Devī* should dwell in 16 forms, in the 16 cities decorated with gems, for the protection of this universe.

Accordingly, those architects constructed 16 cities in the 16 *kṣetrās*. These are on the top of 9 mountains and 7 oceans. These 16 cities were named as *Kāmeśwarī*, *Bagamālāpurī*, etc., based on the names of *Titi Nityās*. Out of these there are three peaks to the East, South-west, South-east and center of *Meru* mountain. In those three peaks there are the residences of *Brahmā*, *Viṣhṇu* and *Śiva* and in the center the residence of *Śrī Devī*.

Śrī city is located above all the *Brahmāṇḍās*, in a peninsula of gems amidst the ocean of nectar. There is many a nursery like multi treed *Mahotdyānam*, *Mandāra Vāṭikā*, *Kalpa Vāṭikā*, *Santāna Vāṭikā*, *Harisanta Vāṭikā*, *Pārijāta Vāṭikā*, *Kadamba Vana Vāṭikā* and so on surrounding this city. Further this city is encircled by different forts made of Iron, Steel, Copper, Lead, Brass, Five Metals, Silver, Gold, Topaz, Sardius, Aromatic, Diamond, Chrysoprase, Indigo Blue, Pearl, Emerald, Coral, Nine Gems and various gems and metals. Also surrounded by different theories like mind, intellect and ego and further surrounded by luster of Sun, Moon and Cupid.

There lies the house of *Chintāmaṇi* in this city. Within this cited is the *Śrī Chakra*. In the center of this on the seat of Five *Brahmas*, on the great throne – on the *Bindu* plank called *Sarvānandamayam* – seated is the great *Mahā Tripura Sundari* gracing us all.

Tantrarāja Tantra (28th chapter) describes şuch a construction of *Śrī* city. *Vidopākyānam* also has details. *Lalithopākyānam*, *Lalitāstavaratnam* and *Chintāmaņi Stavam* may be referred for more details about *Śrī* city and *Chintāmaņi* house.

Tantrarāja Tantra (28th chapter) explains that *Nityā Devīs* are in the form of the worlds and time and their interchange. Accordingly, *Śrī Devī* dwells in the *Mahā Meru* during the first year of *Kruta Yuga* (*Kruta* era). *Nityā Devīs* starting from *Kāmeśwarī* till *Jvālāmālinī* live in other *Jambu Dvīpam*, *Plakśa Dvīpam*, etc., and seven oceans. *Chitrā Nityā* lives in the outside ether. In the next years each *Nitya Devī* (including *Śrī Devī*) moves to the next place. In the same way in the following years they move to adjacent places. In the sixteenth year they return to their original places. Each of the *Nityā Devī*s becomes the Moon of *Meru* in one year. (Further details in this regard can be had from the original book and its commentary called *Manorama*).

<u>784th name</u> – *Prāņarūpiņī* – प्राणरूपिणी;

One breath is to once inhale and exhale. The calculation of time as day, month, etc., is done by breath only. *Titi Nityā Devī*s are in the form of time. Since the time origins from breath, it can be taken as that *Titi Nityā Devī*s are the breath. *Śrī Devī* is also one of the *Titi Nityā Devī*s and hence **She** is *Prāņarūpiņī*. The related verses in *Tantra Rāja Tantra* (27th chapter) may be referred; *Athaşodasa Nityānām Kālena Prāņatochyate*.

<u>22nd verse</u> in *Phalasruti* part of *Śrī Lalitā Sahasranāmam* – On the full Moon day, one should meditate by imagining *Śrī Devī* on the Full Moon, after offering the five oblations and these thousand names should be read. The night of the full Moon day is the last night of bright fortnight of the Moon. This has to be chant in the night only when the full Moon *titi* spans at that time.

On the full Moon day, *Śrī Devī* has to be imagined on the full Moon. All the fifteen *Titi Nityā Devīs* and the 16th *kalā* called *Sādā* also shine in the form of full Moon. The evidence for this is the 240th name *Candramaṇḍalamadhyagā*.

Let us try to understand about each of *Titi Nityā Devīs* individually;

1.   *Kāmeśwarī*;

She blesses us all holding Noose, sugarcane bow, wine vessel, goad, flower arrows and boon signet in hands, red in colour, three eyes[24] and with a crescent moon in the head.

This *Devi's Gāyatrī – Oṃ Kāmeśwaryai Ca Vidmahe Nityakklinnāyai Ca Dīmahe Tanno Nityā Pracodayāt.*

By worshipping this *Devi*, the devotees get the results like – happiness, wealth, peace and liberation.

---

[24] 453rd name in *Śrī Lalitā Sahasranāmam* is *Trinayanā*

2. _Bagamālinī;_

She blesses us all holding in her six hands, Lotus, Red Rose, Noose, bow, goad and flower arrows, sitting on a lotus flower with a smile on her face.

This _Devi's Gāyatrī – Oṃ Bagamālinyai Ca Vidmahe Sarva Vaśaṅkaryai Ca Dīmahe Tanno Nityā Pracodayāt._

By worshipping this _Devi_, the devotees get the results like – attracting all, protection of the womb and success in all tasks.

3. _Nityaklinnā;_

She blesses us all holding in her 4 hands noose, goad, _Abhaya_ (no fear) signet and drinking vessel. She is red in colour, has three eyes and sits in a lotus flower.

This _Devi's Gāyatrī – Oṃ Nityaklinnāyai Ca Vidmahe Nitya Mantrāyai Ca Dīmahe Tanno Nityā Pracodayāt._

By worshipping this _Devi_, the devotees get the results like – co-operation in the family and love and affection.

4. _Beruṇḍā;_

She blesses us all holding in her hands, lotus flower, garland for _japam_, _Abhaya_ (no fear) signet and conch. She is white in colour, has a crescent in her head.

This *Devi's Gāyatrī – Oṃ Beruṇḍāyai Ca Vidmahe Viṭiharāyai Ca Dīmahe Tanno Nityā Pracodayāt.*

By worshipping this *Devi*, the devotees get the results like – health body and satiation of all wises.

5.   *Vahnivāsinī*;

She blesses us holding in her 8 hands – conch, chakra, sugarcane bow, lotus flower, a *kalasam* (pot), noose and goad. She has three eyes and She is in golden colour.

This *Devi's Gāyatrī – Oṃ Vahnivāsinyai Ca Vidmahe Siddhipradāyai Ca Dīmahe Tanno Nityā Pracodayāt.*

By worshipping this *Devi*, the devotees get the results like – health body and satiation of all tasks/ wishes.

6. *Mahāvajreśwarī*;

She blesses us holding in her hands – pomegranate fruit, sugarcane bow, noose and goad. She has three eyes. She is also called as *Bhavāni Mātā*.

This *Devi's Gāyatrī – Oṃ Mahāvajreśwarīyai Ca Vidmahe Vajranityāyai Ca Dīmahe Tanno Nityā Pracodayāt.*

By worshipping this *Devi*, the devotees get the results like – getting rid of all sorrows.

7. _Śivadūtī;_

She blesses us with 8 hands, shining like a Sun.

This *Devi's Gāyatrī – Oṃ Śivadūtyai Ca Vidmahe Śivaṅkaryai Ca Dīmahe Tanno Nityā Pracodayāt.*

By worshipping this *Devi*, the devotees get the results like – getting rid of *adharmas*, benefitting with all types of wealth and protection from danger.

8.   _Twaritā;_

She blesses us holding a noose, a goad, and no fear and boon signets in hands. She wears a snake as a jewel. She has a peacock feather in her head. She is always with a group of bears and lions.

This *Devi's Gāyatrī – Oṃ Twaritāyai Ca Vidmahe Mahānityāyai Ca Dīmahe Tanno Nityā Pracodayāt.*

By worshipping this *Devi*, the devotees get the results like – education, knowledge, wealth and health.

9. _Kulasundarī_;

Her image is a peculiar form. She has 6 faces and 12 hands. She holds a book, coral garland, a stylus, a conch and knowledge and boon signets in hands. She is red in colour and has a young moon on the forehead.

This _Devi's Gāyatrī – Oṃ Kulasundaryai Ca Vidmahe Kāmeśvaryai Ca Dīmahe Tanno Nityā Pracodayāt._

By worshipping this _Devi_, the devotees get the results like – expertise in speech, knowledge, wealth and surrendering of enemies.

10. _Nityā_;

She has 6 faces and 12 hands. Her colour is that of a rising Sun. She holds a goose, goad, sugarcane bow, shield, trident, flower arrow, knife, a skull, book, and no fear and boon signets in hands.

This _Devi's Gāyatrī – Oṃ Nitya Bharaivyai Ca Vidmahe Nitya Nityāyai Ca Dīmahe Tanno Nityā Pracodayāt._

By worshipping this _Devi_, the devotees get the results like – strength of the body and soul and all the eight _Siddhis_.

11. *Nīlapatākā;*

She has 5 faces and 10 hands. Her colour is Blue. She has three eyes. She holds no fear and boon signets in hands. She sits on a lotus flower.

This *Devi's Gāyatrī – Oṃ Nīlapatākāyai Ca Vidmahe Mahā Nityāyai Ca Dīmahe Tanno Nityā Pracodayāt.*

By worshipping this *Devi*, the devotees get the results like – success in examinations and law related issues.

12.   *Vijayā;*

She has 5 faces and 10 hands. Her colour is that of a rising Sun. She is surrounded by various other *śaktis.*

This *Devi's Gāyatrī – Oṃ Vijayādevyai Ca Vidmahe Mahā Nityāyai Ca Dīmahe Tanno Nityā Pracodayāt.*

By worshipping this *Devi*, the devotees get the results like – success in battles/ wars, success in arguments, every type of wealth and pride.

13. *Sarvamaṅgalā;*

She is in golden colour. She has three eyes. The Sun and the Moon are her eyes. She sits on a lotus form *Padmāsanā.*

This *Devi's Gāyatrī – Oṃ Svom Oṃ Sarvamaṅgalāyai Ca Vidmahe*

Chandrādityai Ca Dīmahe Tanno Nityā Pracodayāt.

By worshipping this *Devi*, the devotees get the results like – knowledge, wealth, successful travels and all auspiciousness.

14. *Jvālāmālinī*;

She has 6 faces, 12 hands and three eyes in each face.

This *Devi's Gāyatrī – Oṃ Jvālāmālāyai Ca Vidmahe Jvālāmālinyai Ca Dīmahe Tanno Nityā Pracodayāt.*

By worshipping this *Devi*, the devotees get the results like – attracting everything including wealth and destruction of all sorrows.

15. *Chitrā*;

She has three eyes and in the colour of rising a Sun.

This *Devi's Gāyatrī – Oṃ Vichitrāyai Ca Vidmahe Mahānityāyai Ca Dīmahe Tanno Nityā Pracodayāt.*

By worshipping this *Devi*, the devotees get the results like – all types wealth.

16. *Mahānityā*;

She is *Śrī Lalitā Parameśvarī* called *Śrī Mahā Tripurasundarī*. Also called as *Avyāja Karuṇā Mūrti*. She is surrounded by all the 15 *Titi Nityā Devis*.

This *Devi's mantra* is the very *Pañcadaśī mantra* itself – *Oṃ aim hrīm śrīm aim ka e I la hrīm ha sa ka ha la hrīm souḥ sa ka la hrīm.*

By worshipping this *Devi*, the devotees get the results like – all enjoyments.

The sage *Dūrvāsa* was the son of sage *Adri* and *Anusuyā Devi*. *Dattāreya* was his brother. He installed and worshipped *Kāmākśi* at *Kāñcipuram*. This has been mentioned in a text called *Kāmākśi Vilāsam*. He authored '*Lalitāstavaratnam*', containing 200 verses. In that text, the 31st verse prays about *Śrī Chakram*. That verse reads;

Śrī Chakram Śruti Mūlakośa Iti Te Samsāra Chakrātmakam Vikyātam Tatadiṣṭitākśara Śivajyotir Mayam Sarvataḥ |
Etan Mantra Mayātmikāpi-raruṇamśrī Sundarībir-vrutam Madyebhaintava Simhapīṭa Lalitetvam Brahmavidyā Śive ||

The meaning of this verse is – you are in an auspicious form! It is an all known fact that the *chakra* of yours called *Śrī Chakram* is a kind of root for *Vedas* and a curtain kind for the *Praṇava mantra* '*Om*'. The auspicious torch of *Pañcadaśākśarī mantra*, stated there, is spreading everywhere. The *Āvarṇa Devis*, in the form of *Pañcadaśī* are surrounding you. You in Red colour giantly and valiantly sitting on the throne called *Bindu*. You are in the form of *Brahma Vidyā*.

The root for the *Vedas* is the *Praṇava mantra* '*Om*'. The three sides of the center triangle of the *Śrī Chakram* are *A*, *U* and *M* – the combination is *Om*. The *Bindu* is in this form. The covering of this is the *Śrī Chakram*.

Śrī Chakra Navāvarṇa Pooja has deep philosophical meanings. Sinking deep into it, is an impossible task for any human being. It was earlier mentioned about the *Kamalāmbā Navāvarṇa Kīrtanās* of *Śrī Muthuswamy Dīkśitar*, a great *Śrī Vidyā Upāsakar*. Those *Kīrtanās* are filled with root letters (*bījākśaras*). Even before him, *Ūtthukāḍu Venkata Kavi* also have wrote *Kāmākśi Navāvarṇa Kīrtanās*. It is possible to perform *Śrī Chakra Navāvarṇa Pooja*, by singing these *Navāvarṇa Kīrtanās* alone and get the equal results.

Let Śrī *Lalitā Parameśvarī* surrounded by *Titi Nityā Devi*s, bless all her compassions to all the readers. There is not even an iota of doubt in this.

*****

Śrī Chakra Navāvarṇa Devis

For the word *Āvarṇam*, we can have the meaning as curtain. Worshipping till all the curtains are removed is called *Navāvarṇa* pooja. The 43 triangles have been discussed earlier. Now let us look at the same in a different perspective;

- 9 *Śaktis* – *Icchā, Kriyā, Gnāna, Satva, Rajas, Tamas, Paśyanti*[25], *Madyamā* and *Vaikharī*
- 10 organs – 5 organs of action, Mouth, Feet, Hands, Anus and *Upastam*.
- 5 organs of knowledge – Eyes, Nose, Mouth, Ears and Skin
- 5 *prāṇans* – *Prāṇan Apānan, Vyānan, Udānan* and *Samānan*
- 5 *karāṇas* – mind, intellect, haughty and will
- 5 elements of nature – Ether, Air, Fire, Water and Earth
- 10 sensitivities – sound, touching, form, smell, speech, *gamanam*, rhythm, *vasarggam* and bliss

Lord *Viṣṇu* is present in a *Saḷagrāma*, Lord *Śiva* is present in a *Linga* and in the same way *Śrī Devī* is present is *Śrī Chakra*. Squares, circles, triangles and petals are all seen in a *Śrī Chakra*. Since it has nine *Chakras*, it is called *Navayoni Chakram*. Since it has 43 triangles it is called *tricatvārimśad Chakra*. *Śrī Devī's* *mātrukā śaktis* are present in this Chakra and hence it is called as *Mātrukā Chakram*. It is also called in tantras as *Parama Maṅgaḷa Chakram*, *Śivaśakti Aikya Chakram*, *Sadānanda Sampūrna Chakram* and so on. It has to be kept in the heart, called as *Daharākāśam* and worshipped.

Sri Devi Bhagavatam 12th *Skandam* chapters 10 to 12 describe the *Manidveepam* the dwelling place of *Śrī Devī*. These 9 *Āvarṇa*-s are metamorphically compared to the 9 halls made of nine-gems (each with one gem). These 9 halls are mentioned as surrounding the *Chintamani* house – There shines *Śrī Devī*. All the *Āvarṇa Devīs* detailed below are explained in those chapters.

---

[25] 368th, 370th and 371st names in *Śrī Lalitā Sahasranāma* – *Paśyanti, Madyamā* and *Vaikharīrūpā*

1. First *Āvarṇam* – to integrate
2. Second *Āvarṇam* – to complete
3. Third *Āvarṇam* – to get excited
4. Fourth *Āvarṇam* – to approach/ access
5. Fifth *Āvarṇam* – to carry out
6. Sixth *Āvarṇam* – to protect
7. Seventh *Āvarṇam* – to cleanse
8. Eighth *Āvarṇam* – to accomplish
9. Ninth *Āvarṇam* – to create

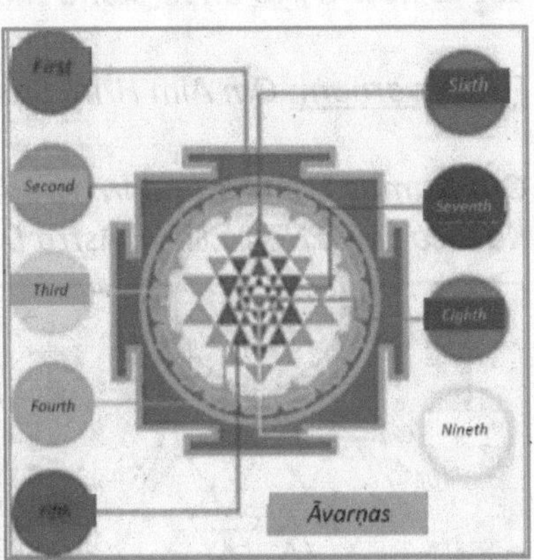

Step by step, crossing all the nine *Āvarṇas*, *Bindu* – unison of *Śiva-Shakti* – the liberation – the super bliss, can be reached. In each of the *Āvarṇas*, *Śrī Devī* is worshipped alongwith her *Āvarṇa Devīs* and at the end of the pooja, *Śrī Devī* is worshipped at *Bindu* and reach the happiness. This is *Navāvarṇa* pooja. In each of the *Āvarṇas*, the concerned *Cakreśwari*, *Mudrū Devī* and other *Āvarṇa Devīs* should be worshipped as prescribed and recommended. Only after their permission, the devotee can step into the next *Āvarṇa*. Only by this method, the devotee reaching the *Bindu*, *Śrī Devī* becomes happy and satiated.

Śrī Chakra Navāvarṇa pooja is considered as a *mahā yagnam*. An enthusiast performing this pooja with devotion gets multi-times benefit than performing *mahā* yagnas like *Vājabeyam*, *Somayāgam*, *Aśvametam*, etc. *Śrī Devī* gets much pleased and bestows her full compassion on this devotee. 230th name in *Śrī Lalitā Sahasranāma* – *Mahā Yāga Kramārādhyā* is worth noting here.

When a beneficiary enters the region, he is getting rid of the world's distractions and conflicts. With more icons and scenes, he is taken to a separate world. Bindu refers to the meeting of the universe called our body and its inherent source.

Let us now try to understand the Devi-s in each of the *āvarṇa*-s.

<u>First *Āvarṇam*;</u> *Om Aim Hrīm Śrīm Aim Klīm Sou:*

Om Namas Tripurasundari, Hrudaya Devi, Śiro Devi, Śikā Devi, Kavaca Devi, Netra Devi, Astra Devi, Kāmeśvari, Baga Mālini,

Nityaklinne, Beruṇḍe, Vahnivāsini, Mahāvajreśvari, Śivadhūti, Tvarite, Kulasundari, Nitye, Nīlapatāke, Vijaye, Sarvamaṅgaḷe, Jvālāmālini, Citre, Mahānitye, Parameśvara-Parameśvari, Mitreśamayi, Ṣaṣṭīśamayi, Oḍyāṇamayi, Caryā Nādamayi, Lopāmurāmayi, Agastyamayi, Kālātāpanamayi, Dharmācāryamayi,

Muktakeśīśvaramayi, Dīpakalānātamayi, Viṣṇudevamayi, Prabhākaradevamayi, Tejodevamayi, Manojadevamayi,

First *Āvarṇam* – First line;

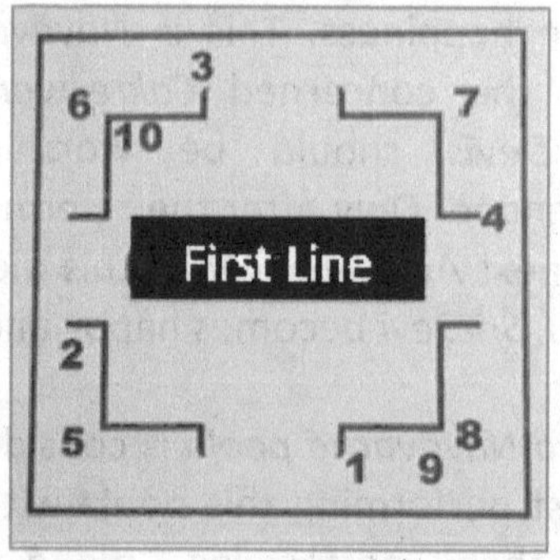

1. *Aṇimā Siddhe,*
2. *Laghimā Siddhe,*
3. *Mahimā Siddhe,*
4. *Īṣitva Siddhe,*
5. *Vaṣitva Siddhe,*
6. *Prākāmya Siddhe,*
7. *Buddhi Siddhe,*
8. *Icchā Siddhe,*
9. *Prāpti Siddhe,*
10. *Mokśa Siddhe,*

First *Āvarṇam* – Second line;

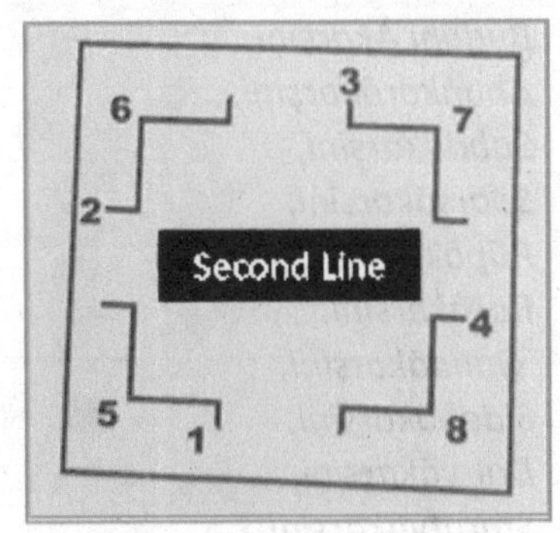

1. *Brahma Śakte – Brāhmi,*
2. *Śveta Varṇe – Māheśwari,*
3. *Śikhi Vāhanā – Koumāri,*
4. *Śyāma Varṇā – Vaiṣṇavi,*
5. *Śyāmaḷā – Vārāhi,*
6. *Śyāma Varṇā – Māhendri,*
7. *Kriṣṇa Varṇā – Cāmuṇḍā,*
8. *Pīta Varṇā – Mahālakśmi,*

First *Āvarṇam* – Third line;

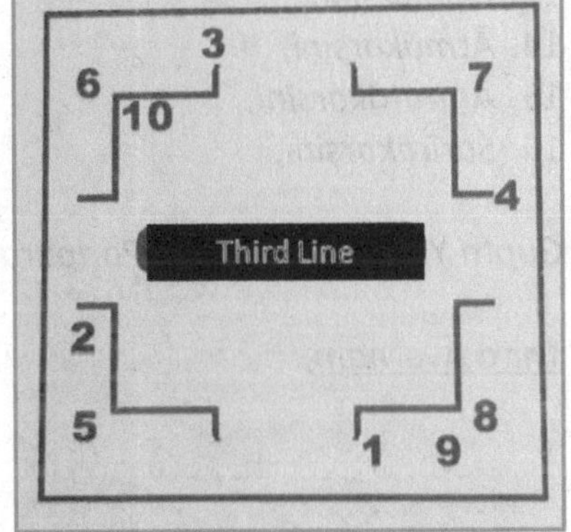

1. *Sarva Samkśobiṇi,*
2. *Sarva Vidrāviṇi,*
3. *Sarvākarṣiṇi,*
4. *Sarva Vaśankari,*
5. *Sarvonmādini,*
6. *Sarvamahānkuśe,*
7. *Sarva Keśari,*
8. *Sarva Bīje,*
9. *Sarva Yone,*
10. *Sarva Trikaṇḍe,*

Prakaṭa Yogini, Bouddha Darśanāngi, Trailokya Mohana Chakrasvāmini,

<u>Second *Āvarṇam*</u>;

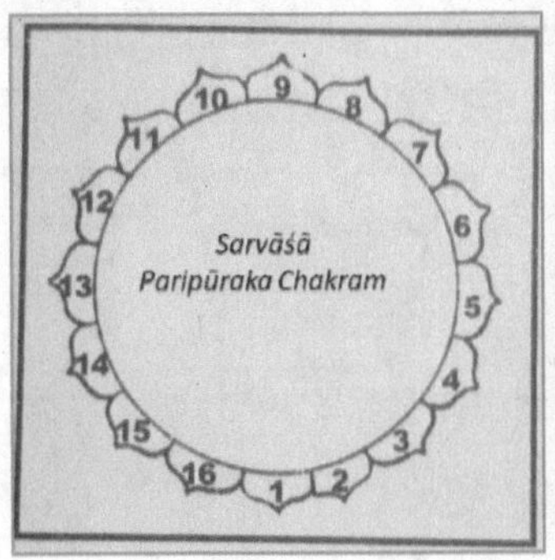

1. *Kāmākarṣiṇi,*
2. *Buddhi Ākarṣiṇi,*
3. *Ahaṅkārākarṣiṇi,*
4. *Śabdākarṣiṇi,*
5. *Sparśākarṣiṇi,*
6. *Rūpākarṣiṇi,*
7. *Rasākarṣiṇi,*
8. *Gandākarṣiṇi,*
9. *Siddhākarṣiṇi,*
10. *Dairyākarṣiṇi,*
11. *Smrutyākarṣiṇi,*
12. *Nāmākarṣiṇi,*
13. *Bījākarṣiṇi,*
14. *Ātmākarṣiṇi,*
15. *Amrutākarṣiṇi,*
16. *Śarīrākarṣiṇi,*

Gupta Yogini, Sarvāvāśā Paripūraka Chakra Svāmini,

<u>Third Āvarṇam</u>;

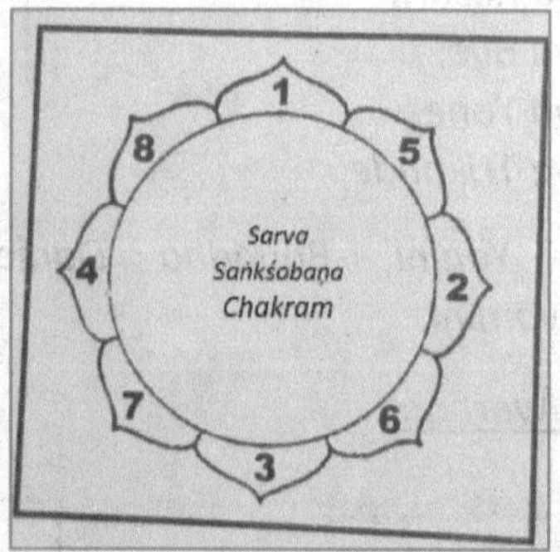

1. *Ananga Kusume,*
2. *Ananga Mekale,*
3. *Ananga Madane,*
4. *Āananga Madanā Ture,*
5. *Ananga Rekhe,*
6. *Ahaṅga Veginī,*
7. *Śanangānguśe,*
8. *Ananga Malini,*

Gupta Tara Yogini, Sarva Saṅkśobaṇa Chakra Svāminī,
Pūrvāmnāya Digdevate, *Sruṣṭirūpe,*

<u>Fourth *Āvarṇam*</u>;

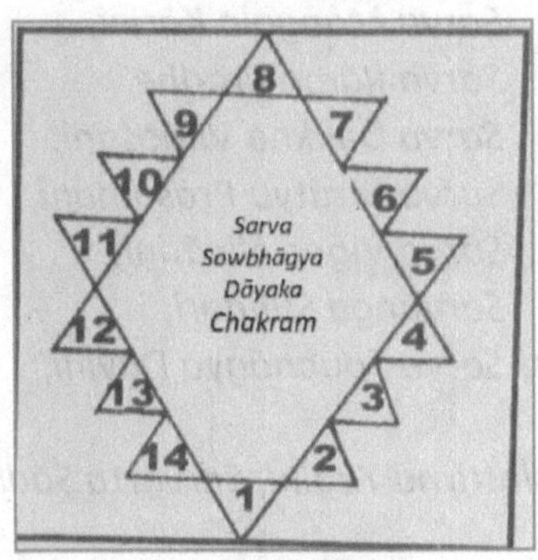

1. *Sarva Saṅkśobiṇi,*
2. *Sarva Vidrāviṇi,*
3. *Sarvākarṣiṇi,*
4. *Sarvāhlādini,*
5. *Sarva Sammohini,*
6. *Sarva Stambini,*
7. *Sarva Jrumbiṇi,*
8. *Sarva Vaśaṅkari,*
9. *Sarva Ranjani,*
10. *Sarvonmādini,*
11. *Sarvārthasādini,*
12. *Sarva Sampatthi Pūrani,*
13. *Sarva Mantramayī,*
14. *Sarva Dvandva Kśayaṅkari,*

Sampradāya Yogini, Sarva Darṣanāṅgi, Sarva Sowbhāgya Dāyaka
Chakra Svāminī,

Fifth *Āvarṇam*;

1. *Sarva Siddhi Pradhe,*
2. *Sarva Sampath Pradhe,*
3. *Sarva Priankari,*
4. *Sarva Mangala Kāriṇi,*
5. *Sarva Kāma Pradhe,*
6. *Sarva Dukkha Vimośani,*
7. *Sarva Mrutyu Praśamani,*
8. *Sarva Vigna Nivāriṇi,*
9. *Sarvānga Sundari,*
10. *Sarva Soubhāgya Dāyini,*

Kulottīrṇa Yogini, Sarvārta Sādaka Chakra Svāminī,

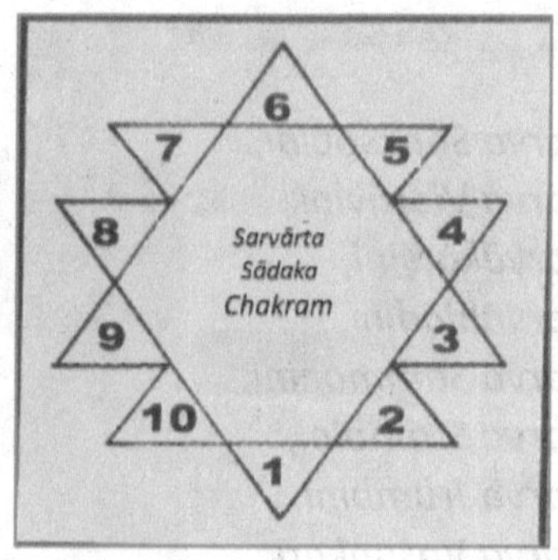

Sixth *Āvarṇam*;

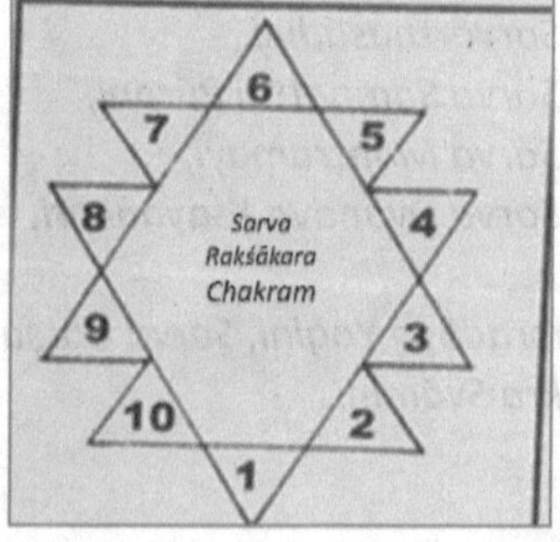

1. *Sarvajne,*
2. *Sarva Śakte,*
3. *Sarvaiśvarya Pradhe,*

4. *Sarva Gnānamayi,*
5. *Sarva Vyādhi Nivāriṇī,*
6. *Sarvādhāra Swarūpe,*
7. *Sarva Pāpahare,*
8. *Sarvānandamayī,*
9. *Sarva Rakśā Swrūpiṇī,*
10. *Sarvepsita Phalaprade,*

Nigarba Yogine, Vaiṣṇava Darśanāṅgi, Sarva Rakśākara Chakra Svāminī,

<u>Seventh *Āvarṇam*</u>;

 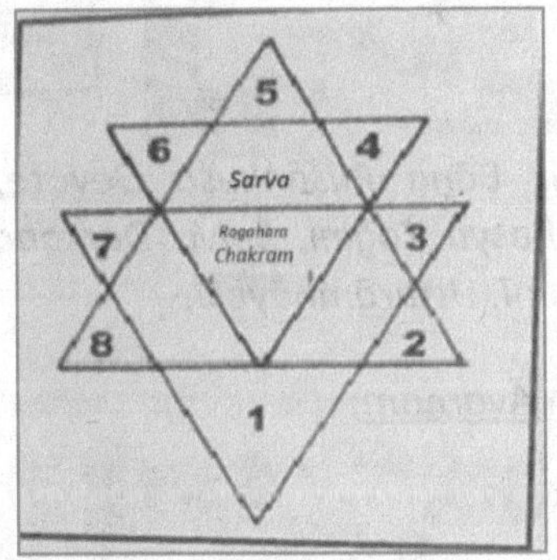

1. *Vaśini,*
2. *Kāmeshi,*
3. *Modini,*
4. *Vimale,*
5. *Aruṇe,*
6. *Jayinī,*
7. *Sarveśvari,*
8. *Koulini,*

Rahasya Yogini, Śākta Darśanāṅgi, Sarva Rogahara Chakra Svāminī, Paścimāmnāyeśi,

<u>Eighth *Āvarṇam*;</u>

1. *Mahābāṇi*
2. *Puśpacāpi*
3. *Puśpapāśi*
4. *Anguśi*

 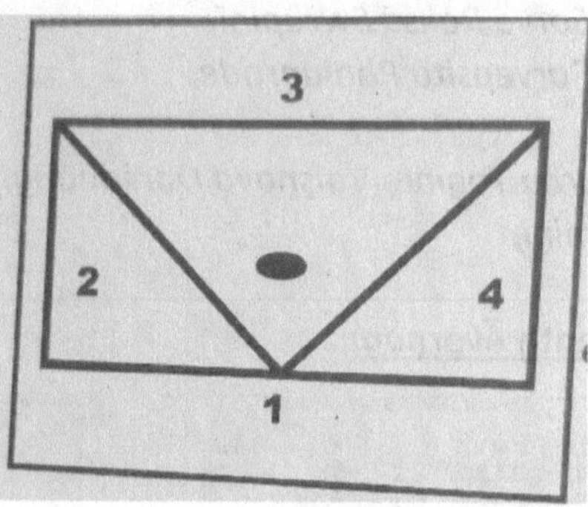

Danur Bāṇa Pāśāṅkuśa Devate, Kāmeśi, Vajreśi, Bagamālini, Atirahasya Yogini, Śaiva Darśanāṅgi, Sarva Siddhiprada Chakra Svāminī, Uttarāmnāyeśi,

<u>Ninth *Āvarṇam*;</u>

 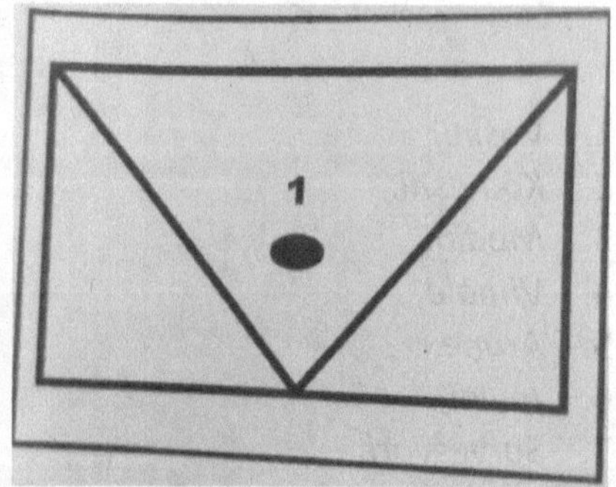

1. *Tripure,*
2. *Tripureśī,*
3. *Tripūra Sundarī,*
4. *Tripura Vāsinī,*
5. *Tripurāśrī:,*
6. *Tripura Mālinī,*
7. *Tripura Siddhe,*

8. *Tripurāmbā,*

9. *Mahā Tripura Sundarī,*

The Sri Chakra Navavarna Puja has a very deep tattvas behind it. It is impossible for anyone to dive into and understand fully. The Kamalamba Navaravana songs sung by Shri Muthuswamy Deekshitar, a great Sri Vidya Upasakar, are embroidered all the root letters (*beejaaksharas*) into them. Even earlier to him, Oottukkaadu Venkata Kavi has sung Kamakshi Navavarna songs.

The various forms of *Ambika* are praised by these Navaravana deities. Let us all realize them and get blessed.

*****

Other Incarnations

In the previous chapters, we learned something about various incarnations of Sri Ambika. Here we will try to find out some other important incarnations that do not belong to any of those groups.

1. *Śrī Mahā Pratyangirā Devī*[26]

Pratyangirā (प्रत्यङ्गिरा) or sometimes called *Nārasimhī* [27] or *Nārasimhikā*, is a Goddess associated with Shakti, the Hindu concept of eternal energy. She is described as a goddess with a lioness's face and a human body. This combination of lion and human forms represents the balance of good and evil.

Appearance of *Pratyangirā Devī*

There are various forms of *Pratyangirā Devī* portrayed by different texts and also specific to the concerned regions. Typical of Lord Narasimha, *Pratyangirā Devī*, who incarnated to pacify him also has a lion face — usually have many arms and many legs in legends and descriptions. She also appears sometimes blue.

In some images she is shown with a dark complexion, ferocious in aspect, having a lion's face with reddened eyes and riding a lion, entirely nude or wearing black garments, she wears a garland of human skulls; her hair strands on end, and she holds a trident, a serpent in the form of a noose, a hand-drum and a skull in her four hands. She is also associated with Bhairava and she has a variant form, namely Atharvaṇa-Bhadra-Kāli.

In some schools in her full form, she is mentioned as humongous, with 1008 heads (symbolically representing the 1008-petalled Sahasrāra Cakra, the universal cakra of cosmic energy) and 2016 hands, riding majestically on a chariot pulled by 4 lions

---

[26] The author of this book has written separate books in Tamil and English on *Śrī Mahā Pratyangirā Devī*

[27] There is another Goddess as *Nārasimhī* — female of Lord *Narasimha*. This Goddess is different form what we are talking about here.

(representing the 4 Vedas), carrying many swords for removing obstacles.

The four lions can be considered to represent - the four *Yugas* (eras); the four stages of one's life - baby, child, adult, elder; the four objectives of human birth - *Dharma*, *Artha*, *Kāma*, *Moksha*; the four stages of spiritual evolution - *Śriyai*, *Kriyai*, *Yogam*, *Gnānam*; and honoured the four divine presences – *Mātā*, *Pitā*, *Guru*, *Deivam* (Mother, Father, Teacher, God). Beneath this chariot was an eight-petal lotus, revealing the path to becoming free from life and birth is the Eight-Fold Path.

The jaws of so many lions make it very powerful for destroying negative karmas, and a great blessing for anyone on a spiritual path. However, such a current can be understandably rough, so it's wise to approach with respect and some consideration of what our heart is asking for.

Here are some of the features and appearance details:

- **Lion face**: *Pratyangirā's* lion face usually protects the good from evil.
- **Thousand heads**: Making the evil fearful; Making the good protected.
- **Two thousand hands**: *Pratyangirā* usually has two thousand hands or arms.
- **Āyudha**: *Āyudha* means weapon in Samskrutam - she has thousands of weapons for destroying the evil.

The below verse explains the form of *Pratyangirā* and also details the weapons held by in her hands.

अक्षमाला, कुण्डिका, पद्म, पानपात्र, बाण, चाप, खड्गचर्म, कुलिश, दण्ड, गदा, शक्ति, चक्र, पाश, त्रिशूल, घण्टा, परशु, शङ्खादि, सहस्रकोट्यायुध धारिणि, शतसहस्रकोटि सिम्हासने, सहस्रवदने, सिम्हवक्ले, ज्वालाजिह्वे, कराळदंष्ट्रे ।

Accordingly, *Pratyangirā Devī* has in her hands;

- अक्षमाला – a garland of beads/ *Rudrākṣa*,
- कुण्डिका – a pot
- पद्म – Lotus flower
- पानपात्र – a vessel with water
- बाण – an arrow
- चाप – a bow
- खड्गचर्म – skin of Rhino
- कुलिश – thunderbolt of Indra
- दण्ड – a rod or stick
- गदा – a mace
- शक्ति – *Śakti* weapon
- चक्र – a disk
- पाश – a snake in the form of a noose
- त्रिशूल – a trident
- घण्टा – a bell
- परशु – an axe
- शङ्खादि – a sword and so on

Her appearance is described as - She is wearing thousand crores of weapons (सहस्रकोट्यायुध) as detailed above, having thousand faces (सहस्रवदने), having lion like teeth (सिम्हवक्ले), having a flaming tongue (ज्वालाजिह्वे) and with a wide tusk (कराळदंष्ट्रे), she is sitting on a throne with hundred thousand crore lions (शतसहस्रकोटि सिम्हासने).

The numbers hundred, thousand and crore should not be taken in literal sense. It should be construed as many - countless.

*****

2. _Sri Kanyākumāri Devī_

The mythological story dates back to the prehistoric Tamil period. *Bana*, a demon by birth was the ruler of his land. He was a very powerful king. He practiced penance and obtained a boon from Lord *Brahma* that his death will only be by an adolescent spinster young girl.

With this powerful boon, he became fearless and wreaked havoc on the entire world. He went on to conquer and oust Lord Indra from his throne. He banished all the *devas* from there. The *devas* who were the personification of the basic natural elements, *Agni* (fire), *Varuna* (water), *Vayu* (air) went uncoordinated and havoc spread in the universe, because Indra (ether) was not able to administer and coordinate the five primary elements.

It is believed that *Bhagavathy*, the unmanifested Prakriti, can only bring order because she is the nature within which everyone lives and hence is unbiased. Bhagavathy manifested herself in the Southern tip of the Aryavartha, to kill Bana and recur the balance of nature. As an adolescent girl, she had immense devotion towards Lord *Shiva*. The Lord decided to marry her. All arrangements were made for the marriage. Lord *Shiva* started the journey from *Sucheendram* for the marriage. The marriage muhurta (auspicious time) was in the early in the morning (dawn). *Narada* made the sound of a cock sending wrong information that the Sun had already risen and the auspicious time passed. The marriage procession returned. Sage Narada realized Bana could only be killed by a young girl and thus interrupted Shiva's marriage with Bhagavathy.

Devi waited for the Lord and finally, she thought that she had been snubbed. With unbearable insult, pain, grief, and anger she destroyed everything she saw. She threw away all the food and broke her bangles. When she finally gained her composure, she undertook continuous penance. Ages later Bana, tried to lure and approach the goddess without realizing who she was. The infuriated Bhagavathy, who was the Bhadrakali herself, slaughtered Bana at once. Moments before his death Bana realized that the one before him was Sakti, the Almighty itself. He prayed her to absolve him of his sins. After killing Bana, Devi assumed her original form of Parvati and reunited with her husband Shiva. Bhagavathy maintained her divine presence in the place, in the Devi Kanyakumari Temple.

Sri Chakra – The Abode of Devi – The presiding image is sported in standing posture with an *Akshamala* in her hands. There is an image of a lion in her pedestal indicating that she is the form of Durga. There is a four-pillar hall in the temple, each of which gives out sounds of Veena (a string instrument), Mridangam (a percussion instrument), flute (wind instrument) and Jalatharanga (porcelain instrument).

The text Tantra Choodaamani says that the Kanyakumari temple is one of the 108 *Shakti Peetas* where the back organ of Sati Devi has fallen.

3. *Grama Devata-s - Village Devis;*

A *grāmadevatā* is the name of the presiding deity or guardian deity (patron deity), usually goddesses, worshipped in villages in India. It is derived from the words *grāma* 'village' and *devatā* 'deity'. Most *grāmadevatās* are village deities who are worshipped solely by inhabitants of that particular village. People, even after migrating from that village continue to worship that deity as a heredity. Hindu deities such as Shiva and incarnations of Vishnu are also worshipped alongside the *grāmadevatās*. They are often worshipped in aniconic forms of the earthenware pots or stones.

Although *grāmadevatās* are most often goddesses, there are a few notable male exceptions. *Dharma-Thakkur* is a god of fertility and disease in West Bengal state of India. Another example is found in *Kala Bhairava*, a fierce form of Lord Shiva in the rural villages of Maharashtra, where he is referred to as Vairavar.

Most Gramadevatas are believed to originate from the pre-Vedic beliefs of indigenous inhabitants of the Indian subcontinent. The worship patterns vary according to region but most do not rely on the *Vedas* and employ non-Brahmins as priests. Unlike Brahminical deities, these village deities will not usually have large temples but have open spaces. A common pattern, especially in South India, is to have a village goddess (a fertility figure) and a guardian and protector of the village at the village boundary.

Possible fertility goddess, Late Harappan — The earliest appearance of the "Mother Goddess" found in South Asia is in Mehrgarh in the form of female terracotta figurines dating to the 4th millennium B.C.E. These figurines are believed to represent the "Mother Goddess". Similar female figurines are found in the 3rd-2nd millennium B.C.E., figures from Harappan civilization sites, including a woman with a plant emerging from her womb and a woman in a tree (believed to be a goddess) being worshipped by another woman, with seven figures below. Due to their association with agriculture, the idea of the earth spirit of *bhumi* is still a common association with villages today just as it was in Harappan times. Evidence of continued veneration of a female village deity comes from a terracotta fragment Chandraketugarh from what is now eastern West Bengal dating to the 1st century B.C.E. The plaque shows a figure holding a parasol, evidently a goddess, being worshipped with earthen pots, fruits, flowers and other offerings similar to those given to modern-day village goddesses. Another group of common iconographies related to *gramadevatas* are the *sapta matrika*, the "seven mothers", which has been discussed earlier. The first mention of these goddesses occurs in the later layers of the Mahabharata dating to the 1st century C.E., and their lack of mention in the Vedas indicates a non-Vedic origin for these goddesses. In addition to the fertility goddesses, the various disease goddesses include deities described with unappealing physical characteristics like *Mariamman* and *Mata*. These goddesses could be represented in the Harappan period by a goddess with weapons in her hair. Similarly, violent goddesses absorbed into Puranic Hinduism, like *Durga*, appear around the 1st century B.C.E., - 1st century C.E. It is very difficult, if not impossible to count the number *gramadevatas*.

Village Gods or Protecting Deities;

Some names to specify - Karuppasamy, Sudalai, Karuppannasamy, Kaathavarayan, Periandavar, Maadan, Muneeswaran, Periasamy, Periannasamy, Iyanar, Malayala Karuppu, Kolli Malai Karuppu, Padinettampadi Karuppu, Ondi Karuppu Sangili Karuppar, Panaiyadi Karuppu, Koothandavar, Samaya Karuppasawmy Kazhuvadiyan, Irulappa Samy, Madasamy, Uttanda Samy, Elllai Karuppu, Madeshwarar, Mahalinga, Rajavayan, Madurai Veeran, Maakaa Muni, Laada Sannasi, Veeraputtira Swamy, Andhra Mudaiyar, Chindambara Nadar, Dadi Veerasamy, Ponnar, Thondi Veeran, Kondarayandi, Vembuli Iyanar, Maruthu Iyanar, Virumandi, Sivalapperi Singaram, Kaliyandi Iyenar, Samanamalai Iyanar, Sirai Meeta Iyenar, Kulathu Iyanar, Veera Muthu Iyenar, Veera Bayankara Iyanar, Kavalkaran, Nondi Karuppu, Manda Karuppu and so on so forth.

Mostly the temples of these Gods will be at the end of the village and hence are called as Ellai Gods (Border deities). Also, from the very names it can be construed that they are installed to protect the villages from evil and all.

To name a few Grama Goddesses or female protecting deities;

Maariamma, Maramma, Kaliyamma, Gangamma, Choudamma, Polimeramma, Kigiramma, Venkali Yaamma, Mariamma, Mysamma, Jadamma, Bossamma, Ellamma, Sheethala Devamma, Etukkai Amman, Kolli Pavai, Paappathi, Karupaayi, Paalamma, Badra Kaali, Poolankondaal Amman, Ponnirathaal Amman, Angala Parameshwari, Kanyakalammaa, Mandaraalamma, Jambulmama, Janamma, Nandai Yalamma, Droupadamma, Annamma, Gouramma, Keluvalamma, Perandalamma, Neeli, Bhairavi, Maadacchi, Ammaachi, Peraatuselvi, Dalavai Phechi, Poonguratti, Pethamma, Manchalamma, Malacisemma, Bhagadavalli, Mankaliamma, Goniyamma, Durgamma, Pappamma, Sunkulamma, Angamma, Thirupadamma, Thirupadam, Angaaramma, Vizhiamaa, Kempamma, Teepaachi Amman, Idaichiamman, Kicchamma, Thotichiamma, Poolamma, Sapta Kannikai, Durgal, Udalamma, Ukkiramaakaali, Ucchina Maakaali, Vaasukodi, Eelamma, Vaanamaalamman, Pechiamman and who not.

The deities like Sudalai Maadan (originated by Goddess Parvati in a cremation ground), Iyyanar, Isakki Amman, Maariamman, Ganesha, Murugan, Valli and others were originally worshipped only in villages. Later when people migrated, these deities became their family gods (*kula deivam*) and people continued to worship these deities by visiting the village frequently.

For majority of the families Goddess Renuka – with some variants in name as Renuka Parameshwari, Mariamma and all will be the *kula deivam*. On the other hand, God Iyyappa – with some variants in name as Iyyanar, Iyyanarappan and all will be the *kula deivam*.

One thing to be keenly noted — the daily pujas in the village temples are not generally manned by Brahmin gurukkals, even if the temple is constructed as per Aagama Shastra. Still Brahmins also worship in these temples treating the God/ Goddess as their family deities.

What is inferred from all these? The deities, once considered as Grama Devata, have become accepted as regular Gods. Also, most of the time the Grama Devatas are goddesses. The reason for the same could be that a mother is the one who gives all the love and affection one needs. Another could be that if you read many of the stories related to the divine, you would realize that most of the demons were destroyed by the female deities. Hence the female gods who went out to destroy the demons were mostly female. This is why most deities are women. There are more temples in the villages for female deities.

They have all been Amman temples. Going one step further, another realization. It is believed that the creator of the universe is the female deity. More importantly, about 90% of them are worship of female deities. Therefore, female deities are considered more powerful than male gods. That is why the goddess of many is the female deity.

Finally, the village goddesses or guardian deities and city deities belong to the same family. That is, everyone is in the divine state. Some of them are worshiped in the same way and some are not. Some are the primary deity in the gods. Some are divine moments, some are angels. This is the reality.

There is no doubt that many of the village goddesses/ clans are various incarnations of Ambika. Kanchi Paramacharya has repeatedly emphasized the importance of family deity in many places. *Gayatri Japa*, repaying the debt to ancestors (*pitrus*) and the worship of the clan deity — without doing any of the three acts of karma or charity, it is strictly said to be of no use.

May we all continue to protect our descendants by continuing our worship to the family deity (kula deivams).

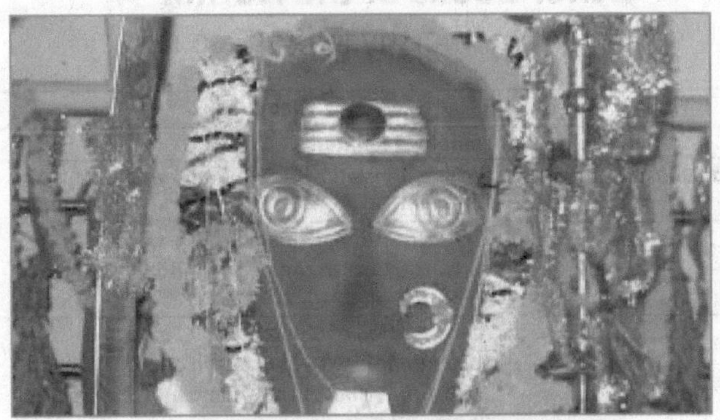

*****

Other Books of the Author
http://ramamurthy.jaagruti.co.in/

#	Title	Remarks	Pages
	Indology Related		
1.	*Shrī Lalitā Sahasranāmam*	English translation of Shrī *Bhāskararāya's Bhāśyam*	750
2.	Power of *Shrī Vidyā*	The secrets demystified – with lucid English rendering and commentaries	80
3.	*Samatā*	An exposition of Similarities in *Lalitā Sahasranāma* with *Soundaryalaharī*, *Saptaśatī*, *Viṣṇu Sahasranāma* and *Shrīmad Bhagavad Gīta*	172
4.	*Advaita* in *Shākta*	Advaita Philosophy discussed in Shakta related Books	80
5.	*Shrī Lalitā Triśatī*	300 divine names of the celestial Mother – **English** translation of *Shrī Ādhi Śaṅkara's Bhāśyam*	193
6.	Secrets of *Mahāśakti*	Chandi demystified	78
7.	*Daśa Mahā Vidyā*	Ten cosmic forms of the Divine mother	60
8.	ஸ்ரீவித்யா பேதங்கள்	ஸ்ரீவித்யா உபாசனையின் படிகள் - கோவை ஶதச் சண்டி மலர்	51
9.	ஸ்ரீ தேவீ ஸ்துதிகள்	பல முக்கிய அம்பாள் ஸ்தோத்ரங்கள்	133
10	Śrī Devī Stutis – श्री देवी स्तुति:	Various important stotras of Sri Devi	
11	ஷண்மத மந்த்ரங்கள் - षण्मत मन्त्रा:	பொள்ளாச்சி ஸ்ரீ ஸஹஸ்ரசண்டி மஹாயாக நினைவு மலர்	145
12	*Śanmata Mantras* - - षण्मत मन्त्रा:	Important Mantras relating to Gods of six religions	87
13	தேவதா மந்த்ரங்கள்	அக்கரைப்பட்டி ஸஹஸ்ரசண்டி மஹாயாக நினைவு மலர்	32
14	ஆதி ஶங்கரரும் ஷண்மதமும்	ஷண்மதங்களைப் பற்றிய ஒரு அறிமுகம்	32
15	ஸ்ரீ ஷண்மத தேவதா அர்ச்சனை	ஸ்ரீ மஹா கும்பாபிஷேக மலர்	64
16	*Vaidhīka* Wedding	Typical Wedding process in English	56
17	வைதீகத் திருமணம்	Typical Wedding process in Tamil	57
18	ஸ்ரீ லலிதா திரிஶதி	300 divine names of the celestial Mother – Tamil translation of *Shrī Ādi Śaṅkara's Bhāśyam*	234
19	ஸ்ரீகுரு பாத பூஜா விதானம்	சித்தகிரி ஸஹஸ்ரசண்டி மலர்	44
20	ஸ்ரீவித்யா ஶ ஈம்னாய மந்த்ரங்கள்	சித்தகிரி ஸஹஸ்ரசண்டி மலர்	60
21	*Ekatā*	Oneness among Shiva, Vishnu and Shakti	277
22	*Vedas* – An Analytical	A description of Veda, Vedanta, Vedanga,	240

#	Title	Remarks	Pages
	Perspective	Jyotisha, Shastra, etc.	
23	*Shrīvidya* Variances	Variances in Srividya Upasana	50
24	வேதங்கள் – ஒரு பகுப்பாய்வு	A description of Veda, Vedanta, Vedanga, Jyotisha, Shastra, etc.	280
25	பரமாச்சார்யாள் நோக்கில் ஸ்ரீலலிதாம்பிகா	The explanation given by Paramacharya on some of the names in Lalita Sahasranama	175
26	*Ṣaṇṇavati* (षण्णवति *Tarpaṇa*	Repaying Debts to Ancestors	42
27	ஷண்ணவதி (षण्णवति தர்பணம்	முன்னோர் கஶன் தீர்த்தல்	48
28	*Shrī Mahā Pratyangirā Devī*	Holy Divine mother in ferocious form	41
29	ஸ்ரீ மஹா ப்ரத்யங்கிரா தேவீ	தெய்வீக அன்னையின் பயங்கர வடிவம்	51
30	*Śrī Chakra Navāvarṇam*	Marvels of *Śrī Chakra*	115
31	ஸ்ரீ சக்ர நவாவர்ணம்	ஸ்ரீ சக்ரத்தின் அதிசயங்கள்	130
32	அம்பிகையின் (திரு) அவதாரங்கள்	ஸ்ரீ தேவியின் பல்வேறு அவதாரங்கள்	142
33	Incarnations of Holy Mother	Different Incarnations of *Śrī Devī*	140
34	ஸ்ரீ பிரணவானந்தர் - ஒரு சரிதம்	ஒரு அரிய ஸ்வாமிகளின் திவ்ய சரிதம்	90
35	ஸன்யாஸம் - ஓர் அலசல்	ஹிந்து மத ஸன்யாஸ பேதங்கள் - ஒரு பகுப்பாய்வு	150
36	Asceticism – an Analysis	A Study of Hindu Sanyasam	150
37	ஶாந்தமும் ப்ரணவமும்	(ஸ்ரீ ஶாந்தானந்தரும் ஸ்ரீ ப்ரணவானந்தரும்) குரு சிஷ்யருக்கு உபதேசங்கள்	120
38	ஶாக்த உபநிஷதங்கள்	ஸ்ரீ தேவியைப் பற்றிய உபநிஷதங்கள்	400
39	*Shakta Upanishats*	*Upanishats* about *Sri Devi*	90
Applied Samskrutam Based			
40	*Paribhāṣā Stora-s*	An exploration of *Lalitā Sahasranāmam*	96
41	*Shrī Cakra*, An Esoteric Approach	Mathematical Construction to draw *Shrī Cakra*	64
42	Number System in Samskrutam	An overview of Mathematics based on Samskrutam	123
43	*Vedic* Mathematics	30 formulae elucidated	146
44	Vedic IT	Information Technology and Samskrutam	162
IT Based			
45	Orthogonal Array	A Statistical Tool for Software Testing	180
Banking Based			
46	Retail Banking	A guide book for Novice	213
47	Corporate Banking	A guide book for Novice	232
48	Dictionary of Financial Terms	A Guide Book for all – Demystifying Myriad Global Financial Terms	215

#	Title	Remarks	Pages
49	GRC in BFS Industry	(Governance, Risk Management and COmpliance by Banking & Finance Industry)	200

Let him be blessed to share his knowledge and experience with others through more books. Let us wish him all the best.

*****

Bibliography

The following books were referred to write this book. Lot many thans to the authors and the publishers. They were very useful.

#	புத்தகத் தலைப்பு	ஆசிரியர்
1.	தெய்வத்தின் குரல் – 7 volumes	ரா. கணபதி
2.	நன்மையளிக்கும் மந்த்ரங்களும் அதன் பயன்களும்	ஸ்ரீ புவநேச்வரி அவதூத வித்யா பீ ம்
3.	ஸ்ரீ சண்டிகையின் சரிதம்	ஸ்ரீ V. அரவிந்த் ஸுப்ரமண்யம்
4.	ஸ்ரீ வித்யா	அண்ணா
5.	Śrīvidyā Koṣa	Prof. S.K. Ramachandra Rao
6.	Other books of the same author.	

Om Tat Sat ॐ तत् सत्

*****

www.ingramcontent.com/pod-product-compliance
Lightning Source LLC
Chambersburg PA
CBHW021809130726
47987CB00010B/3080